# Vocabulary EnergizerS

*Stories of Word Origins*

## David Popkin

# Vocabulary Energizers:
# Stories of Word Origins

## by David Popkin, Ph. D.

*DEDICATION*

For Samuel and Helen Popkin

*Vocabulary Energizers*
© Copyright 1988. David Popkin. All rights reserved.

ISBN 978-0-929166-01-8

Twenty-seventh printing: April 2019.

PRINTED IN THE UNITED STATES OF AMERICA

Hada Publications
2605 Belmont Boulevard
Nashville, Tennessee 37212

# Contents

# ACKNOWLEDGEMENTS

I would like to thank Diana Bach for proving both a patient sounding board and a scrupulous editor. Others who generously helped in various ways are Robert Barzan, Dorothy Chase, David Clark, Bernie Cohen, Ernest Heard, Robert Johns, David Montgomery, Dolores Nicholson, Abba Rubin, Caroline Smith, and Ada Willoughby. Thanks to my wife, Hae Yung, and our children, Joan, Phil, and Dan, for their tolerance and support. Dan and especially Joan assisted with the proofreading. Last but not least, thanks to the Fisk students whose feedback in my vocabulary courses resulted in the conception and development of this text.

D.P.

# PREFACE

Vocabulary texts are too often dull compilations of words and their definitions. Students, initially interested in learning new words, come to associate vocabulary development with word lists, mechanical exercises, and rote memory. What a shame! Many words have fascinating origins and backgrounds. The history or etymology of a word provides a cultural context that helps imprint the word in our memories. Etymologies therefore serve as excellent mnemonic devices that deepen our understanding of a word's nuances and connotations.

For the past four years, I have emphasized narrative etymologies in a vocabulary development course that I introduced at Fisk University. Students learn that behind many vocabulary entries lurk enticing stories; rather than being numbed by word lists that ultimately destroy their incentive to continue vocabulary improvement beyond the confines of the classroom, they awake to the wonder of words. Their interest kindled, students become seekers rather than shunners of new words.

This book, the offspring of my vocabulary course, has three aims: (1) to increase vocabulary, (2) to unveil the origins of words, and (3) to nurture an ongoing interest in words and their backgrounds. In order to help fulfill the third aim, I provide a bibliography of works that I have found especially rewarding and enjoyable in my search for the sources of words.

David Popkin

# TO THE INSTRUCTOR

The format of *Vocabulary Energizers* is ten uniform chapters. Each chapter contains ten core words with their etymological stories. After each story comes the category labelled "Synonyms." In this category I list several words. All but the last of these are easy synonyms for the core word. The last synonym is more difficult and is accompanied by its pronunciation. The first exercise at the end of each chapter is a passage in which the student fills in the blanks with core words. Next comes a matching exercise to reinforce both the core words and the difficult synonyms. I conclude each chapter with a word part from which five difficult but useful words are derived; students then must use these five words in the exercise sentences. Thus, each chapter contains twenty-five words (ten core words, ten difficult synonyms, and five words derived from a word part) for which exercises are provided. In addition, I often include the categories "Related Words" and "Contrasted Words" after "Synonyms." The related words are difficult synonyms or near synonyms for the core word; the contrasted words are difficult antonyms or near antonyms for the core word. Instructors can emphasize whichever of these words they wish. Since many words do not have exact synonyms or antonyms, the instructor can point out the nuances of meaning in the synonyms, related words, and contrasted words. Each chapter is independent from the other chapters so that the instructor is free to select the arrangement of chapters. Master exercises following the last chapter reinforce all of those words which previously were provided with exercises. These master exercises thus serve as a comprehensive review.

# Chapter 1

1. herculean

2. bowdlerize

3. pandemonium

4. pander

5. quixotic

6. cynical

7. stoical

8. stigma

9. impede

10. expedite

1. *herculean* (hur kyuh LEE un, hur CUE lee un) — tremendous in size, strength, difficulty, or effort

Hercules was the greatest and strongest of the heroes from Greek mythology. While still in his cradle, he crushed in his fists two serpents that were sent to kill him. Barehanded, the teenage Hercules slew a lion. Unfortunately Hercules was quick-tempered and, rebuked by his music teacher, slew the teacher as well. The epitome of male virility, Hercules fathered fifty-one sons of forty-nine women in a single night (two of the women bore twins). Hercules was continually plagued by tragedy. Cursed with momentary insanity by the goddess Hera, he killed his three sons by his first wife. He atoned for this act by accomplishing twelve super-human tasks known as "the Labors of Hercules." Hercules' life came to an end when a second and most devoted wife was tricked into giving him a poisonous robe as a present. This robe, spelling instant death for any normal mortal, caused Hercules to feel as if his body were aflame. Too powerful to be killed, he suffered prolonged, excruciating torture. Finally he asked to be burned on a funeral pyre. As the fire rose about him, the gods took pity and flew his soul to heaven.

Today a heavily muscled man such as a champion body builder is said to have a herculean build. Herculean tasks are those which seem almost impossible, such as establishing peace among nations and distributing the world's wealth more equitably so that no one goes hungry. These tasks can only be accomplished through herculean efforts.

*Synonyms:* mighty, powerful, massive, immense, colossal (kuh LOS ul)

*Related words:* titanic, mammoth

*Contrasted words:* frail, puny

2. *bowdlerize* (BOHD luh rize) — remove or change parts considered vulgar or immoral

Today's X-, R-, and probably even some PG-rated films might have caused Thomas Bowdler to have a stroke. For Bowdler, even Shakespeare was too naughty. In 1818 Bowdler prepared an edition of Shakespeare's plays in which "those expressions are omitted which cannot with propriety be read aloud in a family" and are "unfit to be read by a gentleman in the company of ladies." The plays were drastically altered; many passages were changed, and some characters were totally removed. Bowdler's next act of literary butchery was to amputate from Edward Gibbon's *The Decline and Fall of the Roman Empire* "all passages of an irreligious or immoral tendency." Like all censors, Bowdler evidently thought himself uncontaminated by what he felt would contaminate others. His name has become synonymous with prudish censorship. When we read a bowdlerized work, we risk being deprived not only of pleasure but also of literary quality and historical truth.

*Synonyms:* delete, censor, expurgate (EK spur gate)

*Related word:* purge

3. *pandemonium* (pan de MOH nee um) — utter confusion or wild uproar

The seventeenth-century English poet John Milton coined the word "pandemonium" in his epic poem *Paradise Lost*. This poem described the Fall of Adam and Eve and the casting of Satan and the other rebellious angels into Hell. Milton named the capital of Hell "Pandemonium," an apt description since *pan* means "all" and *daimon* means "demon" in Greek. "Pandemonium" is now used in a metaphorical sense for the condition when "all Hell breaks loose." Teachers experience pandemonium when they confront a wild and unruly class, a chaotic situation created by the noisy chatter of "little devils."

*Synonyms:* disorder, chaos, noisy confusion, tumult (TOO mult)

*Related words:* bedlam, turmoil, clamor

*Contrasted words:* tranquility, placidness, serenity

4. *pander* (PAN der) — play up to another's desires and weaknesses

Chaucer, famous for his fourteenth-century classic *The Canterbury Tales*, wrote the long poem *Troilus and Criseyde*, a story about the Trojan War. Troilus was a prince of Troy, Criseyde a young and beautiful widow. Troilus fell in love with Criseyde and asked Pandarus, Criseyde's uncle, to help him get acquainted with Criseyde. After arousing his niece's interest in Troilus, Pandarus arranged for the couple to make love in his home. Because of his morally questionable manipulation of these lovers, Pandarus has given us the word "pander," which as a noun means a "pimp." More commonly used as a verb, the word "pander" means "to cater to one's baser emotions," as when tricky land developers pander to our greed, pornographic movies pander to our lust, and ambitious politicians pander to the uneducated masses for their votes.

*Synonyms:* indulge, gratify, cater (KAY ter)

5. *quixotic* (kwik SOT ik) — idealistic but not practical

The Spanish novelist Cervantes, a contemporary of Shakespeare, created the world-famous novel *Don Quixote*. Don Quixote imagines himself to be a knight who must fight for right and defend the weak. Accompanied by his faithful companion and squire Sancho Panza, Don Quixote engages in wildly impractical feats, such as fighting a windmill he mistakes for evil giants and demonstrating his courage by challenging two enormous lions to a fight. This tall, gaunt, middle-aged, and ultimately lovable knight has become synonymous with the romantic and impractical. Hence, quixotic solutions are visionary and idealistic but unlikely to succeed. Critics of summit conferences think it quixotic that brief meetings of world leaders can bring about lasting peace.

*Synonyms:* romantic, visionary, fanciful, chimerical (kuh MER ih kul)

*Related word:* utopian

*Contrasted words:* mundane, pragmatic

6. *cynical* (SIN ih kul) — doubting the goodness and sincerity of human motives

The ancient Greek philosopher Antisthenes transmitted and elaborated upon the teaching of his master Socrates. Because his mother was not born in Athens, Antisthenes had to conduct his school outside the city of Athens in a gymnasium called *Cynosarges*, meaning "white dog." He taught that virtue was the greatest good and that pleasure, power, and wealth should be scorned. Diogenes, a famous pupil of Antisthenes, used a tub for shelter and sleep to show his contempt for material success. According to legend, when Alexander the Great met Diogenes sunning himself and offered to grant any wish of the philosopher, Diogenes asked Alexander to step aside since he was blocking the sun. Diogenes was also said to go around with a lighted lamp in broad daylight. When questioned why he did so, he replied that he was looking for an honest man, thus implying that such a man was impossible to find. We can probably see how the followers of Antishenes and Diogenes came to be regarded as insolent and contemptuous. Originally the school of thought of Antisthenes became associated with the name of his gymnasium, *Cynosarges* ("white dog"), but eventually those philosophers were associated with the name *cyn* ("dog") because of their dog-like forgoing of human comforts, uncivil currish behavior, and snarling contempt for others. Today a cynic is one who thinks self-interest motivates all action. A cynical person is skeptical and sarcastic. According to the Victorian playwright Oscar Wilde, a cynic is a "man who knows the price of everything, and the value of nothing," perhaps a cynical remark about cynicism.

*Synonyms:* distrustful, sneering, derisive (dih RYE siv)

*Related words:* sarcastic, skeptical, sardonic, pessimistic

*Contrasted words:* credulous, ingenuous, gullible, naive, optimistic

7. *stoical* (STOH ih kul) — indifferent to pain and pleasure

A pupil of the Cynic philosophers, Zeno founded his own school in Athens about 300 years before the birth of Christ. Since he met his students at the *poikile stoa* ("painted porch"), a place famous for its painting of the Trojan War, his teachings became associated with the Greek work for "porch" (*stoa* or *stoikos*). Zeno believed that one should cultivate wisdom by not being concerned with gaining or losing material possessions and by calmly accepting both fortune and misfortune. A stoical person, therefore, shows great self-control, whether confronting pain, pleasure, joy, or grief. The following passage from the Hindu classic the *Bhagavad-Gita* describes a stoic:

> One to me is loss or gain,
> One to me is fame or shame,
> One to me is pleasure, pain.

Shakespeare's Hamlet praises his stoical friend Horatio:

> A man that Fortune's buffets and rewards
> Hast ta'en [taken] with equal thanks; and blest are those

Whose blood [passion] and judgement are so well com-
    meddled [mixed together]
That they are not a pip [musical instrument] for
    Fortune's finger
To sound what stop she please. Give me that man
That is not passion's slave, and I will wear him
In my heart's core, ay, in my heart of heart,
As I do thee [i.e., Horatio].

*Synonyms:* self-controlled, imperturbable (im pur TUR buh bul)

*Related words:* tranquil, impassive, dispassionate, stolid

*Contrasted word:* volatile

8. *stigma* (STIG muh) — mark of disgrace

In ancient Greece captured runaway slaves were branded on the forehead with a *stigma* ("tattoo") to make escape in the future more difficult. When a criminal was stigmatized in seventeenth-century England, he was branded with a hot iron. Slaves in the United States were also branded, as we see Margaret Walker describe in her novel *Jubilee* the brutal searing of a young girl's face. Even after the Civil War, former slaves were stigmatized by much of white society, that is, "marked with disgrace," the modern meaning of the word. Many employers stigmatize ex-convicts as untrustworthy by refusing to hire them. Benedict Arnold bears the stigma of being America's most famous traitor.

*Synonyms:* stain, taint (TAINT)

*Related words:* odium, onus

*Contrasted words:* accolade, tribute

9. *impede* (im PEED) — hinder, obstruct, slow down the process of

10. *expedite* (EK spuh dite) — speed up; hasten or help the accomplishment of

Slaves and convicts in ancient Rome were sometimes shackled with leg-irons. The Latin word *impedio*, coming from *im* ("in") and *pedis* ("foot"), meant "to chain the feet." Today when we are impeded from doing something, we are hindered in our action, though usually not by having our feet tied. A noisy roommate may impede one from studying for exams. Administrative red tape impedes registering for classes. To overcome impediments, we strive to expedite matters, *expedio* in Latin meaning "to release the feet." When the leg-irons were taken off the slaves, they were able to take the "foot" (*pedis*) "out" (*ex*) of its chain.

If we know a college president, he may expedite our acceptance to his institution. Computers expedite problem-solving by releasing us from laborious calculations.

*Synonyms* for "impede": block, delay, retard, thwart (THWORT)

*Related words* for "impede": obstruct, hinder

*Synonyms* for "expedite": accelerate, quicken, facilitate (fuh SIL uh tate)

# WORKING WITH WORDS

*I. Fill in each blank with the appropriate word from the following list:*

|              |              |
|--------------|--------------|
| stoical      | quixotic     |
| impeded      | cynically    |
| stigma       | pandemonium  |
| bowdlerize   | pandering    |
| herculean    | expedited    |

*Each word must be used only once.*

The greatest of all English dictionaries is the multivolume *Oxford English Dictionary, OED* for short. This work defines and dates the first written use of a word and then traces, through a wealth of quotations, how the word has been used over the years. The *OED* thus presents a historical portrait of our English words. The man chiefly responsible for the (1)_____ task of producing this enormous dictionary was the British scholar James A. H. Murray (1837-1915). Some people probably thought such a visionary task was impractical and (2)_____; others (3)_____ thought that no one would undertake such an immense project unless promised a fortune or international acclaim. Murray, however, was not interested in (4)_____ to the masses for a quick reward, but painstakingly labored to produce a work of the highest scholarship despite being (5)_____ by inadequate funding. He would not suffer the dictionary to bear the (6)_____ of failing to meet the most exacting standards. The production of this work was in part (7)_____ by Murray's large family, the children helping with the tedious filing. The (8)_____ present in many large families was absent from Murray's orderly household. Basically self-disciplined, persevering, and (9)_____, Murray rarely complained about his herculean labor. He would have become enraged, however, at any attempt to alter or (10)_____ what he thought essential to the dictionary.

## II. Match the word on the left with its synonyms.

_____1. cynical       a. taint, stain

_____2. bowdlerize       b. tumult, disorder

_____3. expedite       c. chimerical, fanciful

_____4. stigma       d. cater, indulge

_____5. pander       e. expurgate, delete

_____6. stoical       f. colossal, immense

_____7. quixotic       g. imperturbable, self-controlled

_____8. herculean       h. derisive, distrustful

_____9. impede       i. facilitate, accelerate

_____10. pandemonium       j. thwart, hinder

## III. Word Part: VOC — voice, call (vocation, vocal)

*vociferous* (voh SIF ur us) — noisy; loudly insistent

*evocative* (ih VOK uh tiv) — calling up, producing; suggestive

*avocation* (av uh KAY shun) — hobby

*irrevocable* (ih REV uh kuh bul) — unable to be called back or undone; unchangeable

*equivocate* (ih KWIV uh kate) — use words ambiguously or unclearly, usually in order to mislead; hedge

*Using each of the five VOC words only once, complete the following sentences.*

1. My vocation is engineering, my _____ gardening.

2. The _____ crowd demanded its money back when the star performer failed to appear.

3. Don't _____; I want a clear answer immediately.

4. My decision is _____; nothing will make me change my mind.

5. The _____ sea breeze recalled our childhood in Rockaway Beach on the shore of the Atlantic Ocean.

# Chapter 2

| | |
|---|---|
| 1. tantalize | 6. galvanize |
| 2. labyrinth | 7. lethargic |
| 3. Machiavellian | 8. ostracize |
| 4. laconic | 9. gregarious |
| 5. maudlin | 10. egregious |

Quizlet for quiz

1. *tantalize* (TAN tuh lize) — arouse hopes that will be frustrated

In Greek mythology Tantalus was a mortal son of Zeus, king of the gods. Several stories tell how Tantalus enraged the gods. According to one version, Tantalus revealed secrets entrusted to him by Zeus. Another story recounts that Tantalus invited the gods to a banquet for which Tantalus had killed and cooked his only son. Repulsed by this attempt to make them cannibals, the gods punished Tantalus by placing him in a clear pool above which grew delicious fruit. Whenever he sought to relieve his thirst or hunger, the water and fruit would always recede just beyond his reach. The gods repaid Tantalus' horrid banquet by making it impossible for him ever again to feast. To "tantalize," then, is to tease with a desired object that is always kept beyond reach.

    Candy, cake, and pie tantalize the dieter. A famous college football coach might turn down a tantalizing multimillion-dollar offer from professional football because of strong ties to his present community.

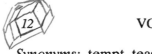 

*Synonyms:* tempt, tease, entice (in TYS)

*Related words:* allure, whet

→ maze

2. *labyrinth* (LAB uh rinth) — complex, intricate network of passages; complicated situation; maze

King Minos of Crete prayed for a sign that he was specially favored. Poseidon, god of the sea, gave Minos a beautiful white bull with the condition that the bull eventually be sacrificed. However, Minos decided to keep the magnificent animal and sacrificed another bull to Poseidon. Angered by the king's selfish action, the sea god caused Minos' wife to fall in love with the white bull. To satisfy her lust, the queen had the master craftsman Daedalus design a lifelike wooden cow into which she could enter. The bull was attracted to this cow, and because it was constructed with an appropriate entrance, the queen was able to make love with the bull. From this unusual coupling, the queen gave birth to a half-bull, half-human child — the Minotaur. Unwilling to kill the queen's child, the king had Daedalus build an intricate maze to confine it. This elaborate prison of passageways was called the Labyrinth. Captives thrown into the Labyrinth were devoured by the monstrous hybrid. Eventually, the hero Theseus came to Crete and slew the Minotaur. He was able to find his way out of the Labyrinth because he had fastened one end of a ball of thread near the maze's entrance. After killing the Minotaur, Theseus then followed the thread in his hand back to its origin. Daedalus himself later angered the king and was imprisoned in the Labyrinth. The resourceful engineer, however, fashioned a pair of wings from the feathers of birds for himself and his fellow prisoner, his son Icarus. They flew out of the maze, but Icarus soared too close to the sun, the wax binding his wings melted, and he fatally plummeted to the sea. Today, people complain that the labyrinth of government is as confusing as Daedalus' Labyrinth. Some readers delight in following the labyrinthine plot of a complex mystery; others get lost in its complicated twists and turns.

*Synonyms:* maze, tangle, conundrum (kuh NUN drum) [specifically means a riddle or puzzle]

*Related word:* intricacy

3. *Machiavellian* (mak ee uh VEL ee un) — unprincipled and crafty

The political theorist Machiavelli (1469-1527) lived in Italy during the Renaissance. In his book *The Prince,* essentially a manual for rulers on how to seize and maintain power, Machiavelli counseled reliance on fear rather than love and advocated lying if necessary, for he thought these methods would strengthen the authority of a ruler. For his practical, non-idealistic, frank advice, Machiavelli has become associated with craftiness, double-dealing, and treachery. Hence, "Machiavellian" means "unscrupulous and cunning" — a term often applied to successful but morally deficient individuals.

Politicians may get elected by using Machiavellian tactics, but only if the public does not suspect them of such Machiavellian maneuvering.

*Synonyms:* cunning, crafty, deceitful, guileful (GYLE ful)

*Related words:* devious, unscrupulous, conniving, amoral

*Contrasted words:* candid, frank, aboveboard

4. *laconic* (luh KON ik) — brief, concise

In ancient Greece the Spartans or Laconians (the city of Sparta was in the province of Laconia) were famous for the hardships they bore as part of their vigorous military training. They endured the cold by wearing only the skimpiest of clothing and sleeping on reeds without any blanket. They were taught to speak briefly and only when necessary. One story tells of a Spartan boy who, while standing for military inspection, harbored a wolf cub under his tunic. Refusing to break the required silence, the boy finally collapsed, his heart devoured by the wolf. When Philip of Macedon (father of Alexander the Great) sent a messenger to Sparta to proclaim, "If we enter your city, we will level it to the ground," the Spartans replied with the single word "If!" This laconic answer proved effective; Philip decided not to invade.

A good way to dismiss salespersons who phone or knock on your door is to reply laconically, "No."

*Synonyms:* brief, to the point, concise, terse (TURS)

*Related words:* succinct, compendious, curt, taciturn

*Contrasted words:* verbose, loquacious, garrulous, prolix

5. *maudlin* (MAWD lin) — excessively sentimental

Jesus cast out seven devils from Mary Magdalene. In medieval and Renaissance England, Mary Magdalene was also thought to be the same Mary who was the sister of Lazarus and the reformed Mary who wept at the feet of Christ. Therefore, Mary Magdalene was a common figure in the religious plays of the period that portrayed the life of Jesus. Because the role of Mary demanded considerable crying and because artists also depicted her with eyes red and puffy from weeping, Mary Magdalene became associated with tearful sentimentality. Her eyes were described by the English poet Richard Crashaw (1613-1649) as

> ... two faithful fountains;
> Two walking baths, two weeping motions,
> Portable, and compendious oceans.

From "Magdalene," which gradually changed in sound to "maudlin," comes our word to describe sloppy sentimentality. Today we refer to anything sickeningly sentimental, such as tear-jerking soap operas and self-pitying drunks, as maudlin.

*Synonyms:* mushy, tear-jerking, mawkish (MAW kish)

*Related words:* bathetic, lachrymose

6. *galvanize* (GAL vuh nize) — startle, excite, shock, electrify

The Italian physiologist Luigi Galvani (1737-1798) noticed that the leg of a skinned frog he was dissecting twitched when touched by his scalpel. The scalpel had become charged by contact with an electrical machine. Because Galvani demonstrated that a muscle could be shocked into movement, his name gave us the word "galvanize," which in a general sense means to "stimulate, arouse, spur on."

Adolf Hitler, Winston Churchill, and Martin Luther King, Jr., galvanized audiences with their oratory.

*Synonyms:* excite, stimulate, animate (AN uh mate)

*Related words:* vitalize, exhilarate

*Contrasted words:* lull, pacify, sedate, tranquilize, stupefy

7. *lethargic* (luh THAR jik) — lazy, sluggish, lacking energy

Ancient Greeks believed that the spirits of the deceased drank from the river Lethe before they could enter Hades, the region of the dead. The drink totally wiped out their earthly memories. Spirits returning from Hades to be reborn in our world (the Greek version of reincarnation) first had to drink from Lethe to erase afterlife memories. Greek physicians named a disease characterized by extreme drowsiness after this river — *lethargia*. Nowadays dull and sluggish individuals (who have "forgotten" any motivating drive or purpose) are described as lethargic.

*Synonyms:* drowsy, torpid (TOR pid)

*Related words:* languid, languorous, indolent, slothful, listless, phlegmatic

*Contrasted words:* animated, vivacious, ebullient

8. *ostracize* (OS truh size) — exclude from society, refuse to associate with, banish

When ancient Athens established its democracy, it tried to protect this form of government by removing the threat of a potential dictator. In a special annual election, citizens cast their ballots for those politicians they thought were becoming so dangerously powerful as to possibly overthrow the government. Anyone receiving more than 6,000 votes was banished from Athens for ten years. For a ballot, a citizen used a piece of pottery or tile called an *ostrakon* on which he scratched the name of the person to be exiled. From *ostrakon* comes our word "ostracize," meaning to "banish" or "exclude."

Neighborhood children sometimes cruelly ostracize a new student in their class; ostracizing the class bully makes better sense.

*Synonyms:* reject, isolate, shun (SHUN)

*Related words:* proscribe, oust

9. *gregarious* (gruh GAIR ee us) — liking the company of others; sociable

10. *egregious* (ih GREE jus) — outstandingly bad

Both these words derive from the Latin *gregis*, meaning "flock" or "herd". A gregarious animal likes to be with others of its kind. For example, wolves and sheep are gregarious since they are pack or herd animals. The lion is the only gregarious member of the cat family, an exception to the other cats who hunt alone. Gregarious persons enjoy the company of others; the solitary loner is not gregarious. "Egregious" derives from the Latin phrase *e grege* ("out of the herd or flock"). Originally, the word was positive, applied to one who stood out or apart from the group because of highly regarded qualities. Thus, the seventeenth-century English philosopher Thomas Hobbes wrote, "I am not so egregious a mathematician as you are," meaning he wasn't so great or outstanding a mathematician as the person addressed. In modern times "egregious" has come to mean standing apart from others in the sense of being exceptionally bad. Stealing from a blind beggar and selling drugs to children are egregious acts.

*Synonyms* for "gregarious": sociable, social, convivial (kun VIV ee ul)

*Related words* for "gregarious": extroverted, affable, amiable, amicable

*Contrasted words* for "gregarious": introverted, solitary

*Synonyms* for "egregious": outrageous, flagrant, (FLAY grunt)

*Related words* for "egregious": gross, rank, atrocious, heinous, execrable, appalling

# Working With Words

*I. Fill in each blank with the appropriate word from the following list:*

| | |
|---|---|
| lethargic | tantalized |
| maudlin | laconic |
| egregious | gregarious |
| ostracized | Machiavellian |
| labyrinth | galvanize |

*Each word must be used only once.*

It was awful trying to get through the (1)_____ of registration my freshman year. I was (2)_____ by the prospect of taking exciting courses but could not enroll because my name was missing from the computer printout through some (3)_____ error. For a moment I thought I was the victim of a (4)_____ scheme to exclude me from college. I tried to explain the situation to a university officer but received a brief, (5)_____ reply to go elsewhere for help. The next officer I met was more talkative but was extremely slow moving and (6)_____. I thought that nothing at all could (7)_____ him to action. Fortunately I am not shy but (8)_____; I confront people quite well. I continued to explain that I felt (9)_____ by the very college from which my parents graduated. Upon learning that my parents were alumni, the official introduced me to the president himself. At the risk of sounding (10)_____, I must admit that I still get a lump in my throat when I recall how the president kindly rectified the situation and then recounted how he had been my father's roommate and had introduced my parents to each other.

## II. Match the word on the left with its synonyms.

___1. laconic              a. entice, tempt

___2. galvanize            b. torpid, drowsy

___3. tantalize            c. guileful, crafty

___4. gregarious           d. terse, concise

___5. ostracize            e. animate, stimulate

___6. labyrinth            f. mawkish, sentimental

___7. maudlin              g. convivial, social

___8. egregious            h. shun, reject

___9. lethargic            i. flagrant, outrageous

___10. Machiavellian       j. conundrum, maze


## III. Word part: SPEC — *look, see (spectator, spectacle, spectacular)*

*specious* (SPEE shus) — seemingly true or genuine but actually false; misleading

*retrospective* (re truh SPEK tiv) — looking back at the past

*introspective* (in truh SPEK tiv) — looking inward at one's own thoughts and feelings

*circumspect* (SIR kum spekt) — cautious, watchful, careful

*prospective* (pruh SPEK tiv) — expected, likely, potential

*Using each of the five SPEC words only once, complete the following senten-ces.*

1. You must be _____ and look at many houses before buying your home, or you may find that you have invested your life savings foolishly.

2. The deceptive politician could convince the crowd of almost anything, but upon reexamining his arguments, I almost always found them _____ and illogical.

3. A _____ U.S. Presidential candidate must have wide media appeal.

4. In his old age my grandfather tended to be _____, often telling us about his youthful adventures.

5. The _____ writer recorded every change of her thought and mood; to read her diary is to relive her inner life.

# Chapter 3

1. mesmerize

2. martial

3. erotic

4. cupidity

5. philistine

6. catholic

7. jeopardize

8. precarious

9. foible

10. forte

1. *mesmerize* (MEZ muh rize) — hypnotize, fascinate

The Austrian physician Franz Mesmer (1734-1815) employed spectacular methods. As music played, Dr. Mesmer would have his patients join hands and form a circle in a dimly lit room. Dressed in the bright robes of an astrologer, Dr. Mesmer would then wave a magic wand and go around the circle, talking to and touching each patient while staring into the patient's eyes. Dr. Mesmer claimed many cures, but an investigating committee, which included Benjamin Franklin, declared the doctor to be a fake. However, Mesmer may have achieved some cures through what we now regard as hypnotism. Thus "mesmerism" was first used to describe the phenomenon that would later be called "hypnotism."

A dynamic speaker can mesmerize an audience; in other words he can captivate and spellbind the listeners as though they were hypnotized. We see this process in Coleridge's famous poem "The Rime of the Ancient Mariner" when an old sailor (the ancient Mariner) stares into the eyes of a Wedding Guest and compels the guest to listen to a lengthy, ghostly tale.

> He holds him with his glittering eye—
> The Wedding Guest stood still,
> And listens like a three years' child:
> The Mariner hath his will.

*Synonyms:* spellbind, captivate, enthrall (in THRAWL)

2. *martial* (MAR shul) — warlike, military, pertaining to the armed forces

Mars, the Roman god of war, corresponds to the Greek god Ares. Mars and Venus (the goddess of love) were lovers. When Venus' husband, the blacksmith Vulcan, learned of his wife's unfaithfulness, he set a trap for the lovers. The blacksmith constructed over Venus' bed a finely woven metal net that would spring over Venus and Mars once they began to make love. Much to their displeasure, Mars and Venus were literally "caught in the act." A powerful, military nation, the Romans had much greater respect for the war-god Mars than did the Greeks, who created the preceding myth about Ares/Mars and his ridiculous entrapment in love. The Romans sacrificed to Mars before battles and after victories. They named the month March after him, a time when the start of fair weather permitted military campaigns to begin. Because the surface of the planet Mars is reddish, the planet was given the name of the bloody god of war. Also from the god Mars derives the word "martial," pertaining to fighting and war, as in the martial arts and the martial music of military bands.

*Synonyms:* combative, militant, bellicose (BEL uh kos)

*Related words:* belligerent, pugnacious, truculent, contentious

*Contrasted words:* pacific, civil, conciliatory

3. *erotic* (ih ROT ik) — pertaining to or arousing sexual love and desire

4. *cupidity* (cue PID uh tee) — greed

The god of love — the Greeks called him Eros, the Romans called him Cupid — is usually pictured today as a winged, chubby infant whose arrows cause people to fall in love. Originally, Eros was portrayed as a handsome young man, the son of Aphrodite, the Greek goddess of love (the Romans called her Venus). When Aphrodite felt jealous of a beautiful girl named Psyche, the goddess told Eros to make Psyche fall in love with the most obnoxious and repulsive creature in the world. Eros, upon seeing Psyche, could not shoot his love arrows into her heart, but instead he fell in love with her himself. He arranged to get Psyche as his own bride. Eros hid Psyche in a secret castle and visited her only in the dark of night, forbidding her to view him by light. By preventing Psyche from ever seeing who he really was, Eros hoped to hide his true identity from Psyche and thus make it impossible for her to reveal their relationship to anyone so that Aphrodite could not learn of the affair. Eventually curiosity overpowered obedience; Psyche lit an oil lamp to see her sleeping husband. Astonished by his beauty, she dropped some oil on Eros. Roused by the burning oil, Eros left Psyche, telling her he could never live with a woman he could not trust. Eventually, however, the couple was reunited, Eros having found it impossible to remain away from his love. The gods made Psyche immortal so that Eros and Psyche could remain together as a divine couple. From Eros we get the word "erotic," which means sexually arousing, as in erotic films and erotic literature. From the god's Roman name Cupid comes the word "cupidity," which also has to do with desire, but desire for wealth rather than sex.

*Synonyms* for "erotic": sexual, passionate, amatory (AM uh tor ee)

*Related words* for "erotic": amorous, amative, aphrodisiac, carnal, erogenous, libidinous.

*Contrasted words* for "erotic": chaste, celibate

*Synonyms* for "cupidity": graspingness, possessiveness, avarice (AV uh rus)

*Related words* for "cupidity": acquisitiveness, avariciousness, rapacity, rapaciousness, covetousness

*Contrasted words* for "cupidity": munificence, philanthrophy, beneficence

5. *philistine* (FIL uh steen) — an uncultured, materialistic person who is indifferent or hostile to artistic and intellectual activities

The Philistines were the archenemy of the ancient Israelites. David slew the Philistine giant Goliath. Samson fell in love with the Philistine beauty Delilah. Delilah continually questioned him as to the source of his strength. At one time Samson lied, telling her that if he were bound with new ropes that were never used, he would lose his strength. Delilah bound him and then called out, "The Philistines be upon thee, Samson." Easily, Samson snapped the ropes. In seventeenth century Germany, a university preacher cited this quotation in his sermon in order to liken the local townspeople to the Philistines. During the week preceding the sermon, the local people had fought with and killed a number of the university's students. From then on, German university students referred to ignorant townspeople hostile to education as *Philisters*, the German word for "Philistines." The nineteenth-century German philosopher Schopenhauer said a philistine was "a man who has no mental needs." The nineteenth-century English poet and critic Matthew Arnold popularized the word in our language when he wrote, "The people who most give their lives and thoughts to becoming rich are just the very people whom we call *Philistines*." Opposed to the gross, materialistic trends in the United States, the great American sociologist W.E.B. DuBois believed higher education could counteract this philistine trend: "The true college will ever have one goal, — not to earn meat, but to know the end and aim of that life which meat nourishes." The TV characters Archie Bunker and George Jefferson are philistines.

*Synonyms:* materialist, barbarian, boor (BOOR)

*Related words:* vulgarian, yahoo, ignoramus

*Contrasted words:* intellectual, intelligentsia, highbrow, connoisseur, literati

6. *catholic* (KATH uh lik) — broad-minded, universal

A catholic individual can appreciate quality and possesses broad understanding and sympathy. "Catholic" derives from the Greek *kata* ("concerning") + *holos* ("whole"), which formed the Greek word *katholikos*, meaning general or universal. We are familiar with the capital "C" form of the word in "Roman Catholic." "Catholic" originally meant all of the Christian believers in contrast to just a specific congregation; "Catholic" then came to mean the accepted doctrine of the Roman Catholic Church. With a small "c," "catholic" refers to someone of universal taste, sympathy, and understanding. Thus someone with catholic taste can appreciate the art, music, literature, and customs of various cultures. Liberal in outlook, the catholic person can accept and understand the viewpoints of different individuals and nations. Of course, there need be no conflict between being Catholic and catholic. A priest may be cultivated, widely-traveled, and broad-minded — in other words, a catholic Catholic.

*Synonyms:* broad, comprehensive, unbiased (un BY ust)

*Related word:* cosmopolitan

*Contrasted words:* parochial, provincial

7. *jeopardize* (JEP ur dize) — put in danger

The French had a term *jeu parti*, which meant "game decided." It was used in gambling, games, and sports when the next move could upset a thus far even contest. Contestants in *jeu parti* were in a risky or uncertain position since they were threatened with defeat. Of course, looked at positively, the contestants could also have an equal chance at victory. However, *jeu parti* entered English as "jeopardy," with its meaning emphasizing the possibility of loss rather than gain.

When patients are on the critical list in a hospital, they are in jeopardy or in danger of losing their lives.  If you don't know how to swim and find yourself in deep water, you are certainly in jeopardy.  Students jeopardize their chances of passing a course when they fail to attend lectures.  If you want peace of mind, don't jeopardize your life savings by investing all of it in risky business ventures.

*Synonyms:* endanger, risk, imperil (im PER ul)

8. *precarious* (prih CARE ee us) — unsafe, risky, insecure

"God helps those who help themselves." In other words, it's better to rely on your own hard efforts than to count on chance or prayer to get through some difficulty.  The ancient Romans must have thought so, as evidenced by their word for "obtained by prayer or begging" —*precarius* — which also meant "risky." Latin *precarius* entered English as "precarious," a legal term meaning "dependent upon the will of another." "Precarious" later came to mean "dependent on anything uncertain," hence "risky."

Skating on thin ice is precarious.  Trapeze artists who perform without the security of a safety net and daredevil motorcylists who wear no protective helmets engage in precarious acts.

*Synonyms:* uncertain, hazardous, perilous (PER uh lus)

*Related words:* vulnerable, problematical, dubious

9. *foible* (FOY bul) — minor or amusing fault or weakness

10. *forte* (FORT,  FOR tay) — strong point

"Foible" and "forte" come from French terms in fencing. The weaker part of the foil — from the middle to the tip — is the foible; the stronger part — from the middle to the hilt — is the forte. One's forte can easily block the thrust of an opponent's foible. Hence, our weaknesses are foibles, our strengths fortes. "Foible" suggests a small or even amusing fault, such as the absentmindedness of a professor, a desire for sweets, the inability to resist a bargain.  In contrast, our fortes are our strong

points, things in which we excel. Walt Disney's forte was creating car-
toons; John D. Rockefeller's forte was making money.

*Synonyms* for "foible": defect, flaw, infirmity (in FUR muh tee)

*Related words* for "foible": quirk, idiosyncrasy, eccentricity, frailty

*Synonyms* for "forte": aptitude, talent, métier (may TYAY)

# WORKING WITH WORDS

*Fill in each blank with the appropriate word from the following list:*

| | |
|---|---|
| martial | erotic |
| foible | forte |
| philistine | cupidity |
| mesmerized | precarious |
| jeopardy | catholic |

*Each word must be used only once.*

When I was a little boy, I was (1)_____ by an exhibition of tae kwon do, a Korean form of karate. I begged my parents to let me study the (2)_____ arts so that I could defend myself from the neighborhood bullies. The walk home from school was indeed (3) _____, for I never knew when I would be challenged to a fight and possibly lose a baby tooth considerably earlier than nature had planned. Not only did I fear bodily harm, but sometimes I felt that my very life was in (4)_____. At last my parents gave their consent for my studying tae kwon do, provided that I pay for the lessons myself. Luckily, the local tae kwon do master was not known for his (5)_____; on the contrary, he had a reputation for being generous and charitable. He was no (6)_____, but had a broad and deep appreciation of the music, art, literature, and philosophy of both Asian and Western culture. Born in Korea, he had come to the United States in his twenties and was now in his sixties. However, at that time I didn't care at all that he was a man of broad, refined, (7)_____ taste; I simply wanted to learn how to fight. After listening to my reasons for learning the martial arts and discovering that my allowance would hardly cover fees, the kindly, compassionate teacher agreed to teach me for nothing if I would clean up the tae kwon do studio after workouts. I studied with him from the time I was ten until I was seventeen so that self-defense, originally my weak point, became my (8)_____. I am eternally grateful to my teacher, whose only

(9)_____ in all the years I knew him was to occasionally sneak off at night to see the latest X-rated (10)_____ movie.

## II. Match the word on the left with its synonyms

____1. erotic | a. enthrall, spellbind

____2. jeopardize | b. unbiased, broad

____3. foible | c. amatory, sexual

____4. cupidity | d. métier, talent

____5. martial | e. boor, materialist

____6. precarious | f. avarice, possessiveness

____7. forte | g. imperil, endanger

____8. mesmerize | h. infirmity, defect

____9. philistine | i. bellicose, military

____10. catholic | j. perilous, uncertain

## III. Word Part: PATH — *feeling, suffering, disease (sympathy)*

*apathetic* (ap uh THET ik) — lacking feeling or interest, unconcerned

*empathize* (EM puh thize) — identify with or fully understand another's feelings and thoughts

*antipathy* (an TIP uh thee) — strong dislike

*pathos* (PAY thos) — quality of arousing pity or sadness

*psychopath* (SYE kuh path) — mentally ill or unstable person, especially
one showing aggressive antisocial behavior


*Using each of the five PATH words only once, complete the following
sentences.*


1. Documentary films about the Nazi concentration camps and the
bombing of Hiroshima contain so much _____
that many viewers shed tears of compassion.

2. Police search frantically for the _____
responsible for the slaying of several young women.

3. In the play *Romeo and Juliet*, Tybalt, discovering Romeo's friend
Benvolio with a drawn sword, expresses _____
toward Benvolio:

> What, drawn, and talk of peace? I hate the word
> As I hate hell, all Montagues, and thee.

4. The father who spanks his son and says, "This hurts me more than it
does you" — and really means it — can _____
with his son's pain.

5. When the English teacher asked an unconcerned student if it were
important to learn words such as " _____,"
the student indifferently responded, "I don't care," thus unintentionally
illustrating the meaning of the word.

# Chapter 4

1. *odyssey* (OD uh see) — long, adventurous journey

The ancient Greeks went to war with Troy to regain Helen, the most beautiful woman in the world. During this Trojan War, which lasted ten years, the Greek Odysseus proved himself the shrewdest of the warriors. Odysseus conceived the plan that ultimately enabled the Greeks to defeat the Trojans. He had the Greeks build a huge wooden horse that was hollow inside and then filled it with many of the best Greek warriors. Those Greeks not in the horse then hid from the view of the Trojans. Seeing only the gigantic horse at their gates, the Trojans thought that the Greeks had departed for their homeland and left the horse as an offering for the gods. They took the horse into their city and celebrated late into the night. When they finally dropped off to sleep, the Greeks emerged from the horse and slaughtered the Trojans.

However, though the war ended, Odysseus' adventures did not. It took Odysseus another ten years to get home. One of his adventures was with a Cyclops, a monstrous one-eyed giant. Odysseus and his men found their way into the Cyclops' cave, but when the Cyclops returned, the giant barred the cave door with a massive boulder that Odysseus and his men could not move. The Cyclops then grabbed two of Odysseus' men, tore off their limbs, and devoured the men, bones and all. Odysseus then devised a plan to get the Cyclops drunk. The intoxicated Cyclops asked Odysseus his name, and Odysseus responded, "My name is Noman." When the Cyclops finally fell asleep from the wine, Odysseus and his men took a sharpened pole and gouged out the giant's eye. Odysseus then tied his men underneath the giant's sheep, which were also in the cave. When morning came, the Cyclops removed the boulder to let out the sheep. The blinded monster felt the back of each sheep for any Greek warriors but never thought to feel underneath. Odysseus — clinging to the underside of the largest ram — and his men thus escaped. Eventually realizing that he had been tricked, the Cyclops called out in agony to his fellow giants, "Noman is killing me." His companions replied that since no man was the cause of his pain, he must be sick and that there was nothing they could do, so they left him alone. Thus, the shrewd Odysseus defeated the Cyclops. The Greek epic the *Odyssey* records many other fascinating adventures. Today, any long, eventful journey is called an "odyssey." Marco Polo underwent an odyssey by land from Italy to China, Christopher Columbus an odyssey by water from Spain to America, and Neil Armstrong an odyssey through space from earth to the moon.

*Synonyms:* wandering, roaming, peregrination (per uh gruh NAY shun)

2. *protean* (PRO tee un) — readily changing form or character

Menelaus was a Greek king and husband of the beautiful Helen — the cause of the Trojan War. After the defeat of Troy, Menelaus, like Odysseus, had a long journey before reaching home. Menelaus wandered for eight years before he met the god Proteus' daughter, who helped him return to his native land. She explained that he must force her father into revealing how to get the favorable winds that would drive Menelaus' ship to Greece. To do so, Menelaus had simply to hold fast to Proteus until the god ceased struggling to get free. Not so simple. Proteus could change into any shape he desired. Seized by Menelaus, Proteus transformed himself into a lion, serpent, panther, boar, stream, and finally a tree. Through it all, Menelaus held tight so that eventually Proteus answered all the king's questions. From Proteus comes our word "protean," meaning "very changeable," "adaptable," "doing many things well." A protean actor can assume various roles — from that of the honest, charming, courageous hero to that of the evil, repulsive, cringing villain. Jackie Robinson was a protean athlete, excelling in track, basketball, football, and baseball; a protean baseball player, excelling at fielding, running, and hitting; and a protean human being, excelling as athlete, public relations figure, and civil rights pioneer.

*Synonyms:* changeable, variable, versatile (VUR suh til)

*Related words:* mutable, mercurial, capricious

*Contrasted words:* immutable, invariable

3. *fiasco* (fee ASS ko) — complete or ridiculous failure

*Fiasco* is the Italian word for "flask" or "bottle." There is an Italian expression *far fiasco* ("to make a bottle"), which means "to make a mess of things," "to flop," "to fail." This expression applies to actors who forget their lines. But what is the connection between "flask" and "failure"? No one knows the origin of the expression *far fiasco*, but one theory states that Italian glassmakers were famous for the perfection of their glass; if they found any flawed glass, they would make bottles out of it. Thus the sense of imperfection or failure was associated with *fiasco* ("bottle," "flask"). Another theory explains that a *fiasco* was a flask with a long neck and a rounded base. Such a bottle could not stand upright unless its base was woven with straw or reeds. Without its matted base, the flask would fall — hence the connection between "flask" and "flop" or "failure." One thing is sure; "fiasco" entered English with the meaning of "complete flop."

My campaign for class president was a fiasco; I received only one vote — my own. Literally and figuratively, the baker whose bread does not rise produces a fiasco.

*Synonyms:* failure, disaster, debacle (dih BAH kul)

*Related words:* miscarriage, abortion

*Contrasted word:* coup

4. *idiosyncrasy* (id ee uh SING kruh see) — personal peculiarity

"Idiot" and "idiosyncrasy" derive from the Greek *idio* ("private," "peculiar," "one's own"). The Greeks referred to an individual who did not hold public office as an *idiotes* ("private person"). Although the word was simply a descriptive term in Greek, when the Romans adopted it in the Latin form *idiota*, the word came to have negative overtones. The Romans thought that the reason an *idiota* chose not to hold office was because he lacked intelligence. Hence today an "idiot" is one with subnormal intelligence. "Idiosyncrasy" comes from the Greek *idio* ("peculiar") + *syn* ("together") + *crasis* ("mixture"). It refers to a private or peculiar mixing together of personal traits. Unlike "idiot," "idiosyncrasy" does not suggest deficiency but merely oddity.

One of my dad's idiosyncrasies is to tug his ear when he asks a serious question. The baseball player Harada Oh — the all-time Japanese home run champion — had the idiosyncratic batting stance of raising one leg high and balancing stork-like on the other leg.

*Synonyms:* oddity, mannerism, eccentricity (ek sen TRIS uh tee)

*Related words:* quirk, caprice, whimsy, anomaly

5. *quintessence* (kwin TES uns) — most essential part or quality; perfect example

According to modern science, there are over one hundred elements. However, the ancient Greeks believed that there were only four — earth, air, fire, and water. They then added a lighter and subtler fifth element, which presumably pervaded the universe and composed the heavens. This fifth element was called *quinta essentia* ("fifth essence") in the Latin of the Middle Ages and was regarded as the essential part of any substance. (The sense of *quint* meaning "fifth" can also be seen in our word "quintuplets," referring to five children born at a single birth). Because this "fifth essence" was the highest or most essential, "quintessence" came to mean in English the "finest," "very essence," "perfect representation." In Christianity, Satan is the quintessence of evil, Christ the quintessence of love. According to the old saying, "Genius is one percent inspiration, ninety-nine percent perspiration," the quintessence of genius is prolonged, intense effort. The heavyweight champion Muhammad Ali asserted he was the quintessential boxer with his famous slogan, "I am the greatest!" Shakespeare's Hamlet speaks of man as the "quintessence of dust":

> What a piece of work is man, how noble in reason, how infinite in faculties; in form and moving how express and admirable, in action how like an angel, in apprehension how like a god: the beauty of the world, the paragon of animals! And yet to me what is this quintessence of dust?

*Synonyms:* essence, model, paragon (PAR uh gon)

*Related words:* epitome, exemplar, pith, marrow

6. *rankle* (RANG kul) — cause bitterness, hatred, resentment

The origin of "rankle" goes back to the Greek word for "eye" (*drakos*). From *drakos* came the Greek *drakon* ("dragon") since dragons had fiery eyes. *Drakon* entered Latin as *draco*, and was then transformed to *dracunculus* ("little dragon"), which meant "ulcer" because a running sore felt like one was being devoured by little dragons. Eventually, the word dropped the initial "d" as it passed through French in the form of *raoncler* or *rancler* to ultimately enter English as "rankle." Thus, we say that a festering emotional or mental irritation rankles.

The reason I don't like Sue is because her stealing my boyfriend still rankles. The poor performance of his football players rankled the coach. Shakespeare's King Lear is rankled by the unnatural cruelty of his daughters when he cries,

> How sharper than a serpent's tooth it is
> To have a thankless child.

*Synonyms:* irritate, anger, exasperate (ig ZAZ puh rate)

*Related words:* fester, vex, irk, rile, chafe, peeve, exacerbate

*Contrasted words:* allay, mollify, assuage, palliate

7. *decimate* (DES uh mate) — destroy or kill a large part of

"Ten" is often a good number. In gymnastics and diving, "ten" signifies a perfect score. From the Latin *decem* ("ten") comes our word "decimal" ("based on ten") and "decade" ("period of ten years"). However, for soldiers in ancient Rome, "ten" could be a most devastating number. The Romans either punished their own rebellious soldiers by killing every tenth man or punished the enemy by killing every tenth captured soldier. The Latin word for this punishment was *decimare*, from which comes our word "decimate." "Decimate" no longer carries the specific meaning of a "tenth" but refers to general widespread destruction and slaughter.

Bubonic plague decimated the European population in the fourteenth century; the atomic bomb decimated Hiroshima. Hopefully, antibiotics and peaceful relations can prevent future decimation on this planet.

*Synonyms:* destroy, slaughter, ravage (RAV ij)

*Related words:* annihilate, exterminate, raze

8. *narcissism* (NAR suh siz um) — extreme self-love or self- admiration

According to Greek mythology, Narcissus was an extremely handsome youth — so handsome that all of the females who saw him longed for his attention, but he would have nothing to do with them. Among those who fell in love with Narcissus was the nymph (female nature spirit) Echo. Echo had been previously punished so that she could only repeat what others said. Since Narcissus would not return Echo's affection, the nymph wasted away until all that was left of her was her repetitive voice — the mythological explanation for the phenomenon of the echo. Finally a curse was put upon Narcissus that he might suffer the same pain he caused others. Looking into a pool, Narcissus became enraptured with his own image. Nothing could distract him from this most captivating reflection. Refusing to eat, Narcissus pined away for his own image until his body disappeared. In his place was a beautiful flower, which today bears his name — the "narcissus." Narcissistic individuals, like Narcissus, are excessively absorbed in themselves. Those of us who spend hours each day gazing at our favorite sight in the mirror are guilty of narcissism. To a certain extent pride, concern for one's appearance, and self-love are virtues; carried to an extreme, they become the vices of selfishness, vanity, and narcissism.

*Synonyms:* self-centeredness, conceit, egoism (EE go iz um)

*Related words:* conceitedness, vanity, egotism, egocentrism

*Contrasted word:* self-abnegation

9. *incumbent* (in KUM bent) — (noun) holder of an office or position; (adjective) holding an office or position; resting as a duty or obligation; required.

10. *succumb* (suh KUM) — give in, give up, yield; die

Both "incumbent" and "succumb" derive from the Latin *cumbere* ("lie down, occupy"). An incumbent is one who lies in or occupies an office. The current mayor running for reelection is the incumbent since she already holds the position. The incumbent has done a good job, so the polls project she will be mayor for a second term. "Incumbent" also means to "lie on" as an obligation. It is incumbent upon lawyers to defend their clients, incumbent upon doctors to treat their patients, and incumbent upon government to serve the public. When we succumb to something, we "lie down" (*cumbere*) "under" (*suc* is a variant of *sub*, "under") it; in other words, we give in or give up to it, or in the ultimate sense, die. Do not succumb to laziness if you want to succeed. Many of us, against our better judgment, succumb to peer pressure. After a long illness, Charlie's father finally succumbed to cancer; funeral services will be held Wednesday. Closely related to "incumbent" and "succumb" are the devilish words "incubus" and "succubus." "Incubus" comes from Latin *in* ("in, upon") and *cubare* ("to lie down"). An incubus was a medieval demon who lay with sleeping women, probably accounting for some unwanted pregnancies. The demonic female counterpart was the "succubus" who lay "under" (*suc*) sleeping men — evidently a rationalization for erotic dreams. It was incumbent upon the medieval monk and nun not to succumb to a succubus or incubus. Today an incubus can mean a heavy burden that lies upon one, such as the incubus of being responsible for both one's parents and one's children when one is the sole provider in the family. "Succubus" — rarely used today — is usually restricted to its fiendish meaning.

*Synonyms* for "incumbent": (adjective) required, compulsory, obligatory (uh BLIG uh tor ee)

*Related words* for "incumbent": mandatory, requisite

*Contrasted words* for "incumbent": nonobligatory, nonrequisite

*Synonyms* for "succumb": submit, surrender, capitulate (kuh PITCH uh late)

*Related words* for "succumb": accede, defer, concede, expire

*Contrasted words* for "succumb": withstand, forbear

# WORKING WITH WORDS

*I. Fill in each blank with the appropriate word from the following list:*

| | |
|---|---|
| decimated | fiasco |
| rankled | quintessence |
| protean | narcissism |
| idiosyncrasies | incumbent |
| odysseys | succumbed |

*Each word must be used only once.*

The life of Alexander the Great (356-323 B.C.) was a series of military (1)_____ that extended his empire from Greece to India. One of his (2)_____ was to carry a copy of the Greek epic the *Iliad* with him, for he regarded the hero of this epic, Achilles, as the (3)_____ of the conquering warrior. While in Egypt, Alexander felt it (4)_____ upon himself to see the oracle of Zeus-Ammon. The oracle prophesied that Alexander would conquer the world. After Egypt, Alexander attacked Persia and (5)_____ the city of Persepolis (all inhabitants were either killed or enslaved) to avenge the Persian burning of Athens, for the memory of the Persian atrocity had (6)_____ Alexander. Although Alexander was the quintessential military strategist and a superb administrator, his (7)_____ nature could change from cool rationality to wild rage, exemplified by his losing his temper and killing a good friend. Not modest in the least, Alexander displayed the height of (8)_____ by proclaiming himself a god and requiring his subjects to worship him. At the age of thirty-three, he (9)_____ to malaria without naming a successor. As a result, his generals fought for and divided Alexander's empire among themselves, thus ultimately turning Alexander's plan of a unified world into a (10)_____.

## II. Match the word on the left with its synonyms.

___1. idiosyncrasy      a. capitulate, surrender

___2. decimate      b. obligatory, required

___3. fiasco      c. versatile, changeable

___4. protean      d. exasperate, irritate

___5. odyssey      e. paragon, model

___6. incumbent      f. egoism, self-centeredness

___7. rankle      g. peregrination, wandering

___8. succumb      h. ravage, slaughter

___9. quintessence      i. eccentricity, oddity

___10. narcissism      j. debacle, failure


## III. Word Part: MAL — bad (malnutrition, malfunction)

*malady* (MAL uh dee) — disease, disorder

*malice* (MAL iss) — ill will, desire to harm others

*malinger* (muh LING gur) — pretend illness or injury to avoid work, chores, duty

*malefactor* (MAL uh fak tur) — evildoer, criminal

*malpractice* (mal PRAK tiss) — failure of professional duty or professional misconduct

*Using each of the five MAL words only once, complete the following senten-ces.*

1. In his Second Inaugural Address, Abraham Lincoln stated that he bore the South no ill will: "With _____ toward none; with charity for all; with firmness in the right...."

2. The doctor who left his scalpel in the patient's stomach was sued for _____.

3. We will never get any work done if you all continue to _____.

4. The average headache is a minor _____, but a migraine headache can be devastating.

5. Police caught the _____ responsible for the burglaries.

# Chapter 5

1. amazon

6. procrastinate

2. iconoclast

7. panacea

3. sardonic

8. capricious

4. supercilious

9. introvert

5. nemesis

10. extrovert

1. *amazon* (AM uh zon) — large, strong, aggressive woman

The Amazons of Greek mythology were a tribe of fierce warrior women. Once a year they would mate with men from a neighboring tribe but would kill or send away the male children produced from this union. To enhance their ability as archers, the Amazons would burn or cut off their right breasts to draw more easily their bows. Hence, comes their name — "Amazon" — from the Greek *a* ("without") and *mazos* ("breast"). One of the feats of Hercules — the greatest hero of Greek mythology — was to bring back the girdle of the Amazon queen Hippolyta. Attracted to Hercules, Hippolyta willingly gave him the girdle, but the other Amazons, seeing Hercules leave with the girdle, assumed he was abducting their queen. When they attacked him, Hercules, mistakenly thinking Hippolyta authorized the assault, slew her. The Amazon River in South America got its name from the Spanish who, while exploring the river, were attacked by what they thought were female Indian warriors. Today, we refer to any powerful women such as muscular female Russian shot putters or huge female body builders as amazons.

The head of our construction crew, Molly Molloy, is a real amazon; she can lay pavement and heave concrete blocks as well as any man.

*Synonyms:* powerful woman, athletic woman, virago (vuh RAY go) [in the sense of a scolding, brawling, ill-tempered woman]

*Related words:* termagant, shrew

2. *iconoclast* (eye KON uh klast) — attacker of traditional or cherished beliefs, institutions, ideas

During the eighth century, there was a bitter struggle in the Byzantine Empire about the use of religious images. Some church leaders thought that artistic representation of holy figures would help believers, especially illiterate ones, in their worship; other church leaders thought that such religious imagery was mere idolatry, that the ignorant masses worshipped the image rather than what it represented. Upholding the latter view, the Byzantine Emperor Leo III outlawed paintings and images in the churches. Because he ruthlessly proceeded to destroy the images, the monks — who opposed him and thought him a tool of Satan — called him an "iconoclast," from the Greek *eikon* ("image," "idol") and *klastes* ("breaker"). By the end of the eighth century, the leaders of the Byzantine Empire took a more tolerant view towards artistic representation of religious figures, and the images or icons were restored to the churches. Rather than one who literally breaks images, an iconoclast today challenges established ideas of society.

Copernicus and Galileo, who opposed the prevailing view of their times when they stated that the earth revolved around the sun, were iconoclastic scientists. Whereas Communist leaders of the Russian Revolution were regarded as political iconoclasts, under the Soviet Union those opposed to Communism were the iconoclasts. Ironically, the iconoclasm of one generation may become the institutionalized beliefs of succeeding generations.

*Synonyms:* revolutionary, rebel, radical, dissenter (dih SEN tur)
*Related word:* nonconformist

*Contrasted words:* assenter, conformist

3. *sardonic* (sar DON ik) — mockingly bitter or scornful; sarcastic

According to ancient legend, a poisonous plant grew in Sardinia, an island off the coast of mainland Italy. This Sardinian plant caused the face of anyone who ate it to be twisted in an agonizing grin. Often the plant proved fatal, so that the victims looked as if they had died laughing. From the horrible grin (called *Sardonios gelos* by the Greeks) caused by this Sardinian plant comes our word "sardonic," meaning "mockingly bitter in the extreme." A sardonic smile is not pleasant and joyful, but cutting and ridiculing. Sardonic comedians heap scornful abuse on their targets. A student may cringe under a professor's sardonic comments, his withering sarcasm.

*Synonyms:* sneering, mocking, contemptuous, derisive (dih RYE siv)

*Related words:* cynical, wry, satiric, caustic, scathing, pungent, jeering, taunting, trenchant

*Contrasted words:* affable, amiable, cordial, deferential, gracious

4. *supercilious* (soo pur SIL ee us) — scornfully looking down on others; disdainfully superior

"Supercilious" comes from the Latin *super* ("over," "above") and *cilium* ("eyelid"). The Latin word *supercilium* meant both "eyebrow" (the part above the eyelid) and "arrogance"; we often raise our eyebrow when contemptuously or scornfully looking down on another. Thus comes our word "supercilious," pertaining to the disdain we exhibit toward those we consider inferior. Conceited snobs have a supercilious air about them. Many people thought the renowned scholar supercilious, but his reserve was due to shyness rather than feelings of arrogant superiority. An often told but false story about Marie Antoinette, wife of France's King Louis XIV, has her ask why her Parisian subjects were angry. Upon being told that they were starving from lack of bread, she superciliously replied, "Let them eat cake."

*Synonyms:* scornful, contemptuous, haughty (HAW tee)

*Related words:* arrogant, condescending, patronizing

*Contrasted words:* submissive, unassuming, obsequious, deferential, unpretentious, subservient

5. *nemesis* (NEM uh sus) — agent of revenge, punishment; difficult or unbeatable opponent; something incapable of being achieved or overcome; cause of one's downfall or undoing

To the ancient Greeks, the goddess Nemesis was as welcome as poison ivy or the tax collector. With her sword and whip, Nemesis — goddess of revenge — would pursue and punish those who had offended the gods. For example, she punished Narcissus, the handsome youth so proud of his beauty that he would have nothing to do with any of his female admirers, by making him fall in love with his own reflection in a pool. Narcissus stared entranced at his image until he wasted away. In present usage, the word "nemesis" often means something that cannot be overcome or proves to be our downfall. Although I like school and do well during regular class periods, examinations are my nemesis; no matter how hard I study, I always panic and do poorly on tests. Superman is the nemesis of criminals. In Hawthorne's *The Scarlet Letter*, the minister Arthur Dimmesdale — who conceals his identity as the father of Hester Prynne's illegitimate child — is plagued by the nemesis of a guilty conscience. If you can't remember the meaning of the word "nemesis," this word will be your nemesis on vocabulary examinations.

*Synonyms:* downfall, destruction, retribution (reh truh BYOO shun)

*Related words:* avenger, retaliation, bane, scourge

6. *procrastinate* (pro KRAS tuh nate) — put off till later

"Procrastinate" comes from the Latin *pro* ("for") and *cras* ("tomorrow"). When we procrastinate, we put off for tomorrow what we can do today. Faced with a difficult assignment, many of us spend more time procrastinating than it would to complete the assignment. If we procrastinate too long about accepting a job offer, we may find the job filled by someone else. Shakespeare's Hamlet, who continually delays revenging his father's murder, is a great procrastinator.

*Synonyms:* delay, postpone, defer (dih FUR)

*Related words:* dawdle, tarry, temporize, loiter

*Contrasted words:* accelerate, expedite

7. *panacea* (pan uh SEE uh) — remedy for all desires, sufferings, troubles

Asclepius was the Greek god of medicine. When the ancient Greek philosopher Socrates was condemned to death and made to drink the poison hemlock, his deathbed words were, "I owe a cock to Asclepius," meaning that he was thankful to Greek medicine for at least providing a poison that caused a pain-free death and wished to show his gratitude by having a cock or rooster sacrificed to Asclepius. Asclepius had a daughter, Panakeia, literally meaning "all-healing" (*pan* means "all" as in "Pan-American"). Panakeia was appropriately named since she was the goddess of healing. The Romans gave her name to a plant, the *panacea*, which supposedly healed all diseases. Entering the English language, "panacea" assumed the meaning of a cure-all or universal remedy.

At election time, many candidates sound as if they have panaceas for the public's problems. While proper nutrition and exercise may not be panaceas for all that ails you, they do improve the quality of life. Some people think money is the panacea for everything.

*Synonyms:* universal remedy, cure-all, nostrum (NOS trum)

*Related words:* elixir, sovereign remedy

8. *capricious* (kuh PRISH us) — changeable, unpredictable

Fittingly, the etymology of "capricious" involves unpredictable change. The word derives from *capriccio* ("shivering"), from *capo* ("head") and *riccio* ("hedgehog"); when we shiver from fear or excitement, our hair stands up as if it were the hair of a hedgehog. Then by chance, *capriccio* became associated with the word *capra* ("goat"), as in Capricorn, the astrological sign of the goat. This association led to our word "capricious," meaning "flighty," "impulsive," "jumping about from one thing to another." Thus "capricious" no longer carries the suggestion of our hair jumping up in fear but of our behavior and moods jumping about like a frisky goat. A "caprice" is a "whim" or "fancy." To "caper" is to "leap about playfully" or to "go on a carefree adventure."

I find it difficult to keep up with my daughter's capricious moods. If you want an ordered, steady, predictable career, don't enter the capricious worlds of fashion designing, the stock market, or politics.

*Synonyms:* impulsive, flighty, whimsical (WIM zih kul)

*Related words:* erratic, mercurial, fickle, wayward, vacillating

*Contrasted words:* steadfast, staid, staunch, unwavering, invariable, resolute

9. *introvert* (IN truh vurt) — one who is concerned mainly with self-examination and one's own inner life rather than with others

10. *extrovert* (EK struh vurt) — one whose interests and thoughts are mainly with other people and things outside oneself rather than with one's own inner life

Three Europeans of the early twentieth century enormously influenced psychology and psychiatry: Sigmund Freud (1856-1939), Alfred Adler (1870-1937), and Carl Jung (1875-1961). Early in their careers Adler and Jung worked with Freud, the founder of modern psychoanalysis. Whereas Freud emphasized our underlying drive for pleasure and Adler our underlying drive for power, Jung theorized that our deeper levels of unconsciousness possess a certain wisdom shared by all humanity.

Jung therefore studied the religion and mythology of various cultures. He introduced the terms "introvert" and "extrovert" (from the Latin word elements: *intro* = "within," *extra* = "outside," *vert* = "turn") to classify psychological types. The introvert turns within for satisfaction and support whereas the extrovert turns outward to others for fulfillment. Ideally, healthy persons harmoniously balance the introvert and extrovert within themselves.

My son is a shy, retiring introvert who likes to be by himself; on the other hand, my daughter is an exuberant extrovert who likes nothing better than going to parties. The boss wants extroverted salespersons, not introverts who shy away from customers.

*Synonyms* for "introvert": shy person, self-observer, self-scrutinizer (SELF SKROO tuh nye zur)

*Related word* for "introvert": introspective person

*Synonyms* for "extrovert": socializer, outgoing person, gregarious (gruh GAIR ee us) person

*Related words* for "extrovert": congenial person, affable person

# WORKING WITH WORDS

I. *Fill in each blank with the appropriate word from the following list:*

| | |
|---|---|
| sardonic | superciliously |
| nemesis | iconoclastic |
| capricious | extrovert |
| introvert | panacea |
| amazon | procrastination |

*Each word must be used only once.*

My swimming coach — with her broad shoulders, muscular legs, and assertive manner — was a true (1)_____. I dreaded my daily two-hour practices that began at 5:30 each morning. However, my mother — herself a former Olympic swimming champion — would tolerate no (2)_____ so that I was always on time for every workout. If I ever complained about feeling tired, my coach would sarcastically reply with such biting humor that I felt it would be better to drown than suffer her (3)_____ wit. Her remarks would have made a bold, confident (4)_____ cringe, but they were especially painful to a shy (5)_____ like myself. I longed for some gentle encouragement, some recognition, even some sign of friendly companionship from the coach — for after all, weren't we all ultimately part of the same team? But my proud, scornful coach always viewed me (6)_____, as if I were some insignificant nuisance that she must tolerate. Once, when I incorrectly performed a flip turn, she screamed that I was her (7)_____, the perpetual thorn in her side that frustrated all her attempts at teaching. Unable to endure her abuse, I tearfully complained to my mother. Knowing that I wasn't a flighty, (8)_____ girl but basically serious and disciplined, my mother met with the coach and explained that although swimming was good, my competing in the Olympics would not be a (9)_____ for the world's ills. Perhaps because my mother was a famous champion, the coach had felt pressured to make me one also. After their meeting, the coach eased up, became at times even friendly, surely (10)_____ behavior in the days when it was commonly believed the harder and tougher the coach the better. Now as an adult I may not be a world record holder, but thanks to my mother and yes, my coach, I love swimming.

II. *Match the word on the left with its synonyms.*

___ 1. sardonic

___ 2. nemesis

___ 3. capricious

___ 4. extrovert

___ 5. procrastinate

___ 6. introvert

___ 7. panacea

___ 8. amazon

___ 9. iconoclast

___ 10. supercilious

a. nostrum, cure-all

b. dissenter, rebel

c. self-scrutinizer, shy person

d. derisive, mocking

e. virago, powerful woman

f. haughty, scornful

g. retribution, downfall

h. whimsical, flighty

i. gregarious person, socializer

j. defer, postpone

III. *Word Part: BENE* — *well, good (beneficial, benefit)*

*benediction* (ben uh DIK shun) — blessing, especially at the end of a
   religious service

*benevolent* (buh NEV uh lunt) — desiring to do good; kind, generous

*beneficiary* (BEN uh FISH ee er ee) — person who receives benefits

*benefactor* (BEN uh fak tur) — person who gives help or financial aid

*beneficence* (buh NEF uh sunce) — goodness, kindness


*Using each of the five BENE words only once, complete the following sentences.*

1. In detective stories, a likely murder suspect is the _____
of the insurance policy of the victim.

2. In Charles Dickens' *A Christmas Carol*, three ghosts visit the mean,
miserly Ebenezer Scrooge and help transform him into a
_____, generous person.

3. At the end of the church  service, the minister delivered the
_____.

4. The flood victims were provided with food and shelter due to the
_____ of their neighbors.

5. Some unknown _____ donated five million dollars to our college.

# Chapter 6

| 1. aegis | 6. succinct |
|----------|-------------|
| 2. auspicious | 7. prevaricate |
| 3. jaded | 8. aloof |
| 4. atone | 9. jovial |
| 5. lewd | 10. saturnine |

1. *aegis* (EE jis) — protection, sponsorship

Zeus, the most powerful of the Greek gods, was nursed as an infant by a goat. Since the adult Zeus covered his shield with this goat's skin (*aigis* is Greek for "goatskin"), which made the shield invulnerable, Zeus' shield was known as the aegis. Zeus entrusted his favorite daughter Athena — who miraculously was born full grown from his head — with the aegis. When Zeus or Athena shook the aegis, panic would overcome their enemies. Whereas the aegis protected Zeus and Athena, nowadays "aegis" refers to protection in general.

Our ambassadors are under the aegis of the United States government. We saw a program on good nutrition presented under the aegis or sponsorship of the dairy industry.

*Synonyms:* guardianship, support, patronage, auspices (AW spuh suz)

2. *auspicious* (aw SPISH us) — favorable, promising a good outcome

The word "auspicious" derives from the Latin *avis* ("bird") and *specio* ("see"). The ancient Romans believed that the flight, feeding habits, and songs of birds foretold the future. The Romans even dissected birds, for they thought the birds' internal organs predicted events. The priests who observed the birds were called *auspices* ("bird watchers"). If all the signs were good, then the occasion would be *auspicius*, meaning "favorable" or "of good omen." Hence, today if a young writer produces a well-reviewed best seller, his career is off to an auspicious or promising start. A student who gets all "A's" in his/her first semester has an auspicious beginning in college. Bright sunrise, fragrant flowers, and melodious birds are auspicious of the wonderful day to come. Etymologically related to "auspicious" is the word "auspices." If you are under someone's auspices, you have their favor, support, or sponsorship.

*Synonyms:* promising, encouraging, propitious (pruh PISH us)

*Related words:* opportune, felicitous, providential

*Contrasted words:* ominous, inauspicious, ill-omened, baleful

3. *jaded* (JAY did) — wearied, dulled, or bored by having too much

A line from an old song goes, "The old gray mare, she ain't what she used to be." This old female horse must have look jaded, since "jaded" means "worn-out." In fact, the word "jaded" derives from tired, worn-out horses. Norse *jalda* meant "mare." English sailors visiting Iceland, where Old Norse was spoken, were dismayed by the sight of overworked, underfed horses. *Jalda* entered English as "jade," a term for a weary, worn, worthless horse. The adjective "jaded" was then extended to have the general meaning of overused and exhausted. Today, we often apply "jaded" to a situation of overindulgence. Someone who parties all evening may have a jaded look the next morning. Many Americans are so jaded with sweets, spices, and refined foods, that they have no appetite for a wholesome diet. Children jaded with an overabundance of toys cannot appreciate any gift.

*Synonyms:* worn-out, overindulged, satiated (SAY shee ay tid)

*Related words:* sated, glutted, surfeited, cloyed

4. *atone* (uh TONE) — make up (for a wrong)

Originally, "atonement" meant "at-one-ment" with God, in other words reconciled or in peaceful harmony with God. From "atonement" came the verb "atone," which at first meant to "be at one" or "be in agreement." Since centuries ago "one" was pronounced like our word "own," "atone" (from "at one") is pronounced "uh TONE." Today, when you atone, you are sorry and try to make up for an error, fault, or wrongdoing. The man who broke into the old lady's home later atoned for his crime by repairing her fence and painting her house free of charge. In Charles Dickens' *A Christmas Carol*, Scrooge atones for his past miserliness by becoming the most generous and charitable of men. On Yom Kippur, the Jewish day of atonement, Jews fast and pray that God will forgive their sins. When Henry David Thoreau, the nineteenth-century American author of *Walden*, was asked on his deathbed whether he had made his peace with God, he replied, "I didn't know we had quarreled"; evidently Thoreau felt no need for atonement.

*Synonyms:* make amends, make reparations, expiate (EK spee ate)

*Related words:* redeem, do penance, propitiate, conciliate, recompense

5. *lewd* (LOOD) — obscene, indecent, lustful

"Lewd" comes from Old English *laewede*, meaning "lay" or "not of the church." Since a thousand years ago learning was almost solely associated with the church, anyone who was lewd was thus not of the clergy and most likely ignorant and illiterate. Thus "lewd" acquired the meaning of "unlearned." The upper classes haughtily used "lewd" to refer to what they regarded as the ill-mannered and wicked ways of the ignorant masses. By the time of Chaucer in the fourteenth century, "lewd" had degenerated to its present meaning of "obscene, sexually indecent."

Lewd songs have indecent sexual overtones. Some fastidious

readers of Chaucer's *The Canterbury Tales* might regard the comic sexual episodes as lewd. Having led a relatively sheltered life, a young lady may be shocked by the lewd remarks and behavior she encounters on the first day of her new job.

*Synonyms:* vulgar, smutty, lascivious (luh SIV ee us)

*Related words:* bawdy, ribald, licentious, lecherous, libertine, pornographic, prurient, risqué, unchaste, salacious, scurrilous, wanton

*Contrasted words:* chaste, virtuous, prim, prudish, unsullied

6. *succinct* (suk SINGT) — briefly and clearly expressed

The ancient Romans wore a loose garment, somewhat like a long shirt, called a tunic. This garment was kept in place by a girdle or sash (*cinctura* in Latin). When the Romans wanted to shorten their tunics so as to move more freely, they would tuck up the tunic under the *cinctura*. Thus "succinct" comes from *suc* (a variant of *sub*, "under") and *cinctura* ("girdle"). Today, "succinct" no longer refers to tucking in our garments but to tucking in our words to make our statements short and precise. On his desk, President Harry S. Truman had a sign saying "the buck stops here" — succinctly stating that he would assume all responsiblility and not shirk or shift it elsewhere. Teachers of freshman composition continually tell their students to cut out wordiness and be succinct. In *Hamlet*, Shakespeare ironically has the verbose Polonius praise succinctness: "Brevity is the soul of wit."

*Synonyms:* brief, concise, terse (TURS)

*Related words:* curt, laconic, compendious

*Contrasted words:* discursive, prolix, verbose, circuitous

7. *prevaricate* (prih VAR uh kate) — stray from the truth; mislead

"Don't give me crooked answers" and "don't speak with a forked tongue" are ways of saying "don't prevaricate." "Prevaricate" derives from Latin *varicus* ("straddling") which came from *varus* ("bent"), a term applied to a knock-kneed or crooked-legged person who did not walk straight. The Romans metaphorically extended this concept of crookedness in their word *praevaricator* for a lawyer who secretly agreed with his client's opponent to betray the lawyer's client in court. Hence the modern meaning of "prevaricate" is to "hedge," "straddle," "deceive," "lie." Prevarication usually suggests more of evasion or avoidance of the truth than does direct, outright lying.

In order to know who is truly responsible for the mismanagement of his business while he was away, a boss must cut through the prevarications, falsehoods, and deceptions of those left in charge. Government officials prevaricated during the Senate hearing in order to cover up their illegal actions. John — a prevaricator and procrastinator — will never give you a straight answer as to why he is always putting things off till later.

*Synonyms:* lie, misinform, equivocate (ih KWIV uh kate)

*Related words:* misrepresent, falsify, dissemble

8. *aloof* (uh LOOF) — reserved, detached, unconcerned

Aloof individuals keep their distance, as if they were steering away from the concerns of others. Etymologically, this makes sense. "Aloof" comes from *a* ("towards") and the Dutch word *loef* ("to windward"). "Aloof" thus derives from a nautical term meaning to head the ship into the wind so as to keep distance from the shore. Therefore, it follows that aloof individuals steer away from others.

Some persons may appear cold and aloof although in reality they are merely shy. Doctors often give the impression of aloofness, for they have to maintain a certain objectivity and emotional distance from their patients. Whenever my brother and I quarreled, my father would usually not interfere but stand aloof to let us settle our own differences.

*Synonyms:* removed, unresponsive, uninvolved, indifferent (in DIF ur unt)

*Related words:* standoffish, inaccessible

*Contrasted words:* gregarious, compassionate, sympathetic

9. *jovial* (JO vee ul) — full of hearty humor and fun; jolly

10. *saturnine* (SAT ur nine) — gloomy, grave

The first Greek gods were the Titans. Foremost among these Titans was Cronus, whose Roman name is Saturn. Saturn ruled uneasily, for he learned of a prophecy that he would be dethroned by one of his children. In order to prevent this catastrophe, Saturn swallowed his first five children as soon as they were born. However, his wife tricked him with the sixth child. Instead of giving Saturn the child, she handed him a large stone wrapped in infant's clothing, which he swallowed. This sixth child, called Zeus by the Greeks and Jupiter or Jove by the Romans, grew up to force Saturn to vomit forth the other children. Remarkably, they all emerged unharmed. With the help of his newly released brothers and sisters, Jove overthrew Saturn and made himself king of the gods. Having come to a sad end, Saturn later gave his name to the planet Saturn. Because the planet Saturn is so far from the sun, it was thought to be a cold, gloomy planet, and astrologers noted those born under the sign of Saturn were disposed to gloom. Today we refer to a sour, gloomy character as saturnine. Jove, on the other hand, went on to joyfully lord the heavens. Astrologically, persons born under the sign of Jupiter (the planet named after Jupiter or Jove) were presumed to be joyful and good-humored, hence our adjective "jovial."

My boss never smiles; he is the gloomiest, most saturnine man I know. His jovial wife, however, is always in high spirits. No one would hire a frowning, saturnine man to play the part of jovial, jolly Santa Claus.

*Synonyms* for "jovial": merry, cheerful, jocular (JOCK yuh lur)

*Related words* for "jovial": jocose, jocund, mirthful, blithe

*Synonyms* for "saturnine": moody, sulky, morose (muh ROHS)

*Related words* for "saturnine": dour, sullen, glum, somber, melancholy, funereal, surly, dismal, lugubrious, pessimistic

# Working With Words

*I. Fill in each blank with the appropriate word from the following list:*

| | |
|---|---|
| auspicious | saturnine |
| jovial | atones |
| aegis | aloof |
| succinctly | prevaricate |
| jaded | lewd |

*Each word must be used only once.*

In Charles Dickens' *A Christmas Carol,* Ebenezer Scrooge does not waste words on the Christmas holiday, (1)_____ reacting to any mention of it with the words "Bah!" and "Humbug!" He is a sour, gloomy, (2)_____ old miser, for whom money has an obscene, almost (3)_____ attraction. As he reaches his house on Christmas Eve, he meets the moaning ghost of his deceased business partner, Marley, who is imprisoned by chains linking padlocks, keys, and money-boxes. Marley points out that Scrooge also is imprisoned by greed. Marley's visit hardly seems an (4)_____ sign for the coming of the Christmas holiday. After Marley leaves, three spirits visit Scrooge. Under their (5)_____, Scrooge journeys to look anew at his past, present, and future. Scrooge awakes the next morning and does not deceive, (6)_____ or lie to himself that the spirits were mere dream fantasies; instead, he recognizes that they were revelations about the state of his soul. Acting accordingly, he (7)_____ for his former stinginess by giving generously to the poor. No longer is Scrooge an (8)_____, isolated figure at Christmas. He becomes the most (9)_____ and merry of men, magically rekindling the Christmas spirit in even the most worn-out and (10)_____ souls.

**II. Match the word on the left with its synonyms.**

___1. prevaricate     a. satiated, worn-out

___2. jovial     b. indifferent, unresponsive

___3. saturnine     c. lascivious, vulgar

___4. aegis     d. auspices, support

___5. atone     e. morose, sulky

___6. lewd     f. jocular, merry

___7. aloof     g. propitious, promising

___8. succinct     h. expiate, make amends

___9. auspicious     i. terse, concise

___10. jaded     j. equivocate, lie

**III. Word Part: EU — good, well (the name "Eugene" means "well born")**

*eulogy* (YOO luh jee) — speech or writing in praise of someone or something, especially of one who has died

*euphemism* (YOO fuh miz um) — pleasant, mild, or inoffensive expression substituted for an unpleasant or offensive one

*eugenics* (yoo JEN iks) — science of improving a breed or species (especially human beings) through selection of parents

*euphoria* (yoo FOR ee uh) — feeling of complete well-being, great happiness, bliss

*euthanasia* (yoo thuh NAY zhuh) — mercy killing; painlessly putting to death someone suffering from a prolonged and incurable condition

*Using each of the five EU words only once, complete the following sentences.*

1. We practice _____ to improve farm animals and plants but shy away from controlling the heredity of human beings.

2. The incurably ill patient requested _____ rather than lingering on as a human vegetable.

3. In Shakespeare's *Julius Caesar*, Mark Antony stands before the corpse of Caesar and says, "I come to bury Caesar, not to praise him," but nonetheless delivers a _____.

4. "Passed away" is a _____ for "died."

5. The actor was filled with _____ when he learned that he had been selected to star in a Hollywood film.

# Chapter 7

1. curtail

2. travesty

3. scruple

4. havoc

5. mentor

6. haggard

7. utopian

8. mercurial

9. diffident

10. hypocrisy

1. *curtail* (kur TAIL) — shorten, reduce, lessen

The tale behind this word concerns a tail. "Curtail" comes from an English word no longer used — "curtal" — meaning a "horse with its tail cut short." "Curtal" itself derives from Latin *curtus* ("short"). Through association with a horse's tail, "curtal" came to be spelled "curtail" and assumed the generalized meaning of to "cut short." While suffering from the flu, I had to curtail my activities. Because I was given only five minutes to speak, I had to curtail the lengthy talk that I had prepared. "Curt" meaning "rudely short or abrupt" also comes from Latin *curtus*. When I asked Judy for a date, she curtly replied "No!" and hung up the phone. I hope I am not being too curt with you, but I must now curtail this etymology with one last brief note: remember, "curtail" derives from a horse's tail and not a cur's (dog's) tail.

*Synonyms:* cut, decrease, diminish (duh MIN ish)

*Related words:* abbreviate, abridge, retrench, truncate

*Contrasted words:* amplify, augment, protract

2. *travesty* (TRAV uh stee) — ridiculous imitation

"Travesty" derives ultimately from Latin *vestire* ("to dress, clothe"), coming to English from the French *travestir* ("to disguise by taking on someone else's clothing"). Today, "travesty" has shed its literal sense of clothing but maintains the metaphorical sense of dressing up or presenting something ridiculously. "Travesty" can be used as a verb as when comedians travesty political leaders, making these serious figures appear absurdly comic. As a noun, "travesty" means a "ridiculous representation," as when incompetent teachers and unruly students make a travesty of education, corrupt judges and bribed witnesses make a travesty of justice, and unloving, frustrated couples make a travesty of marriage.

*Synonyms:* mockery, joke, parody (PAR uh dee)

*Related words:* caricature, burlesque, spoof, lampoon, mimicry, farce, satire, sham

3. *scruple* (SKROO pul) — doubt or uneasiness as to what is right or proper

When ancient Romans walked in their sandals, they were very aware if a small, sharp stone (*scrupulus* in Latin) became caught in their sandals. Because they were bothered by this *scrupulus*, *scrupulus* also assumed the meaning of "anxiety" or "doubt." Just as their soles were made uneasy by sharp stones, so, metaphorically, were their souls made uneasy by the sharp irritation of conscience. Similarly, today we use "scruple" in the sense of moral hesitation or doubt as to what is right. The doctor had no scruple in prescribing the dangerous medicine because he knew that the only alternative to the medicine was death. Often the word "scruple" is used in its plural form, as when we say some man has no scruples for he will lie, cheat, and steal in order to get what he wants. I still have some scruples so I will not sell defective merchandise no matter how profitable. A scrupulous person pays careful attention to detail. My scrupulous camp counselor would never allow us to go to breakfast before we brushed our teeth, put away our clothes, and made our beds so tightly that a coin would bounce on them. Whereas a scrupulous reporter will record everything exactly as it happened, an unscrupulous reporter may change the facts for his/her own advantage. "Unscrupulous" means "without principles or conscience." Clever, unscrupulous people may not have "lost their marbles," but they have lost the stones that prick their consciences.

*Synonyms:* conscience, principle, misgiving, qualm (KWAHM)

*Related word:* compunction

4. *havoc* (HAV uk) — great destruction or confusion

In the Middle Ages, "Havoc!" was a war cry signaling a victorious army to loot and rape in a conquered town. Shakespeare used "havoc" in this sense when he had Mark Antony say in the play *Julius Caesar* that the spirit of the murdered Caesar shall "Cry 'Havoc!' and let slip the dogs of war." In other words, Caesar's spirit will unleash destruction and slaughter. This horrible war cry "Havoc!" was finally outlawed by England's Richard II in the fourteenth century. Recent hurricanes have caused havoc along the Florida coast. Three or four disruptive students can cause havoc in a classroom.

*Synonyms:* ruin, damage, devastation (dev uh STAY shun)

*Related word:* calamity

*Contrasted words:* restitution, reparation

5. *mentor* (MEN tur) — wise, trusted teacher or counselor

When Odysseus — crafty hero of the Greeks who conceived the idea of the Trojan horse — went to fight in the Trojan War, he left his wife and infant son in the charge of his trusted friend Mentor. Since Odysseus did not return ten years later with the other Greeks after the war ended but remained away for still another ten years, many thought he was dead. Hordes of suitors came to ask his wife Penelope to marry them, but she kept putting them off. Mentor could not prevent this rowdy bunch from eating Odysseus' livestock, drinking his wine, and molesting the servants. Finally, Athena — goddess of wisdom and protector of Odysseus — assumed the form of Mentor and told Odysseus' son Telemachus to seek his father. This wise counsel, of course, came from Athena rather than Mentor. Nevertheless, Mentor's name has become synonymous with wise, loyal, and protective guardianship.

Socrates was the mentor of Plato, Plato the mentor of Aristotle, and Aristotle the mentor of Alexander the Great. Another famous mentor was the wizard Merlin, the teacher and protector of King Arthur. American playwright Lorraine Hansberry (1930-1965), famous for her drama *A Raisin in the Sun,* gratefully acknowledged her mentor, the inspiring high school teacher who introduced her to the plays of Sean O'Casey and William Shakespeare.

*Synonyms:* instructor, guide, preceptor (prih SEP tur)

*Related words:* guru, pedagogue

*Contrasted words:* disciple, protégé, ward

6. *haggard* (HAG urd) — looking worn and tired

"Haggard" entered the English language meaning a "wild hawk captured after it had already grown its mature feathers." Since this hawk had a wild, often hungry appearance, the word "haggard" came to be applied to persons looking careworn, exhausted, unhealthily thin and wasted. Shakespeare uses "haggard" in its original meaning when he has Othello say of his wife Desdemona,

> If I do prove her haggard,
> Though that her jesses were my dear heartstrings,
> I'd whistle her off and let her down the wind
> To prey at fortune.

At this point in the play, Othello, racked with jealousy about Desdemona's possible unfaithfulness, says that if he proves her "haggard" (a wild hawk — thus an unfaithful wife), he would tear the "jesses" (straps fastened around a hawk's legs to control it) to release her even if these jesses were attached to his heart. In other words, Othello would send her away even though it would tear his heart out.

Today, a student who stays up all night studying for examinations would most likely have a haggard look the next day. Although they are superb athletes, most marathon runners appear lean, worn, and haggard. These lines from Thomas Hood's "The Song of the Shirt" describe a haggard, overworked seamstress,

> With fingers weary and worn,
>    With eyelids heavy and red,
> A woman sat, in unwomanly rags,
>    Plying her needle and thread.

*Synonyms:* careworn, weary, fatigued, gaunt (GAWNT)

*Related words:* emaciated

*Contrasted words:* robust, hale, jaunty, exuberant

7. **utopian** (yoo TOH pee un) — characteristic of an ideal society; visionary

The Englishman Thomas More (1477-1535) wrote a book *Utopia*, which described a perfect society with justice and equality for everyone. There is no money or private property and everything is solved by reason. Of course, such a society is nowhere to be found, as reflected in the title *Utopia*, formed from the Greek *ou* ("no") and *topos* ("place"). More himself was an incorruptible idealist. Rather than go against his conscience, More refused to support King Henry VIII's divorce and was beheaded. In 1935 the Roman Catholic Church declared More a saint.

Any visionary plan for a perfect society or system can be characterized as utopian. Utopian dreamers may envision the perfect society, but practical realists know that we can only work toward but never achieve the ideal. Each individual has his/her own idea of utopia in his/her view of heaven.

*Synonyms:* idealistic, imaginary, impractical, unfeasible (un FEE zuh bul)

*Related words:* chimerical, quixotic, infeasible

*Contrasted words:* dystopian, anti-utopian

8. *mercurial* (mur KYOOR ee ul) — changeable; unpredictable; lively

The Roman god Mercury, called Hermes by the Greeks, was the messenger of the gods. His winged sandals enabled him to deliver messages with lightning speed. Crafty and sly, Mercury was also regarded as the protector of thieves. Once Zeus/Jupiter, the king of the gods, told Mercury to kill the hundred-eyed Argus. Relying on wit rather than might, Mercury approached the creature of a hundred eyes and told him a series of such dull and monotonous stories that one by one all of Argus' eyes drowsily closed. Then Mercury slew him. The slippery element Mercury, the only metal that is a liquid at room temperature, is named after this sly and slippery god. Because the planet Mercury orbits more swiftly around the sun than any other planet, the Romans named this planet after the swift-footed Mercury. Today, a lively, sprightly, quick-witted person is said to be mercurial. Shakespeare's Mercutio (named after Mercury) in *Romeo and Juliet* is known for his mercurial wit, as is the English writer Oscar Wilde (1854-1900), famous for such remarks as, "The only way to get rid of a temptation is to yield to it." "Mercurial" also means "changeable and unpredictable in mood."

Your temperament is so mercurial; your moods are more changeable and unpredictable than the weather. Who would have thought that my temperamental, moody, mercurial little girl would have matured into a calm, understanding, self-controlled businesswoman, wife, and mother.

*Synonyms:* unstable, high-spirited, impulsive, erratic (ih RAT ik)

*Related words:* capricious, fickle, protean, volatile, ebullient

*Contrasted words:* immutable, stolid, saturnine

9. *diffident* (DIF uh dent) — lacking self-confidence; timid; unassertive

"Diffident" comes from Latin *dis* ("not") and *fidere* ("trust"). Originally, "diffident" meant "mistrustful," as in this seventeenth-century quotation from the *Oxford English Dictionary*: "I am somewhat diffident of the truth of these stories." However, "diffident" came to have the meaning of mistrust in oneself. Therefore, "diffidence" is the opposite of "confidence" (*con* = "with," *fidere* = "trust"). "Fido" is an apt name for "man's best friend," since we have faith or trust in our dog. Diffidence prevented the young man from asking girls for dates. He was a diffident speaker, too frightened to speak in any large assembly. Since you have worked hard, do not be diffident; be confident; ask the boss for a raise.

*Synonyms:* shy, insecure, timorous (TIM uh rus)

*Related words:* coy, demure, self-effacing

*Contrasted words:* brazen, impudent, audacious

10. *hypocrisy* (hih POK ruh see) — pretending to be what one is not, especially to have feelings, beliefs, or virtues that one does not have

Hypocrites play a part pretending to be what they are not. Etymologically, this is appropriate since in ancient Greece the word for actor was *hypokrites*. Hoping to get a better grade, hypocritical students fake concern for a teacher. A hypocrite will smile and compliment you to your face, then criticize and abuse you to others. Molière (1622-1673), the greatest French comic dramatist, made religious hypocrisy the target in his play *Tartuffe*. Introducing himself to a wealthy family, the character Tartuffe pretends to be pious and moral, all the while trying to get rid of the son, seduce the mother, marry the daugther, and imprison the father.

*Synonyms:* deceptiveness, dishonesty, insincerity, deceit, duplicity (doo PLIS uh tee)

*Related words:* pretense, cant, sham, chicanery, charlatanry, sanctimony, sanctimoniousness

*Contrasted words:* candor, candidness, probity

# Working With Words

*I. Fill in each blank with the appropriate word from the following list:*

| | |
|---|---|
| havoc | scruples |
| travesty | haggard |
| utopia | diffident |
| mentor | curtail |
| mercurial | hypocrites |

*Each word must be used only once.*

When our president Mr. Jones first came here, our company was in a severe state of deterioration; many of our laborers were incompetent and most of our managers were corrupt. In fact, our corporation was a joke or (1)_____ at the expense of the shareholders. At first, many were fooled by Mr. Jones since he had a mild, almost (2)_____ manner. However, we soon learned that Mr. Jones was a man of strong moral character; his (3)_____ would not allow him to tolerate any dishonest transactions. Furthermore, he could see through the pretenses and lies of the (4)_____ surrounding him. He caused (5)_____ among the managers, replacing them with men of integrity. (6)_____ laborers who could not consistently perform well also found themselves without a job. However, after some months, Mr. Jones looked careworn and (7)_____. His doctor told him he must (8)_____ his activities to transform his corporation into a perfect system or (9)_____. Fortunately, after a brief vacation, Mr. Jones returned to us in good health. Our company has since been productive, profitable, and ethical. Mr. Jones is a (10)_____ to us all in how to run a business.

## II. Match the word on the left with its synonyms.

___1. mentor              a. erratic, unstable

___2. travesty          b. gaunt, weary

___3. curtail            c. unfeasible, impractical

___4. hypocrisy        d. devastation, ruin

___5. mercurial        e. duplicity, insincerity

___6. diffident        f. parody, mockery

___7. scruple           g. diminish, decrease

___8. haggard           h. preceptor, instructor

___9. havoc             i. timorous, shy

___10. utopian        j. qualm, misgiving

## III. Word Part: MONO — one, single ("monosyllable" means "word with one syllable")

*monologue* (MON uh log) — long speech by one person

*monogamy* (muh NOG uh mee) — marriage with only one person at a time

*monotonous* (muh NOT uh nus) — tiresome because lacking variety; repetitiously dull *monotheism* (MON uh thee iz um) — doctrine or belief that there is only one God

*monopoly* (muh NOP uh lee) — total control of a product or service; company that has this total control; exclusive control or possession of anything

*Using each of the five MONO words only once, complete the following sentences.*

1. My job is boring, dull, and _____; I yearn for variety and adventure.

2. Why do we practice _____ when our biblical ancestors often had more than one wife?

3. My teacher says he welcomes class discussion, but once he starts speaking, the class turns into a _____ with no one else participating.

4. Whereas Hindus worship many gods, Christians, Jews, and Muslims practice _____, worshipping only one God.

5. By eliminating all competitors, we now have a _____ on our product.

# Chapter 8

| | |
|---|---|
| 1. zealous | 6. chagrin |
| 2. candid | 7. cant |
| 3. posthumous | 8. ephemeral |
| 4. enthrall | 9. dexterous |
| 5. parasite | 10. sinister |

1. *zealous* (ZEL us) — extremely active, eager, devoted

"Zealous" comes from the Greek word *zelos*, meaning "intense and passionate devotion or enthusiasm," a meaning still retained in our word "zeal" (ZEEL). During the first century A.D., there was a group of Jews called Zealots, who actively opposed Roman rule. From Masada, a rock-fortress overlooking the Dead Sea, the Zealots fought off the Romans for nearly two years. When defeat seemed inevitable, the Zealots, rather than surrender, committed mass suicide. These passionate Zealots gave their name to our word "zealot" (ZEL ut), meaning a "person excessively enthusiastic or even obsessively and fanatically devoted to a cause."

In order to encourage my son in his studies, I bought him a computer after his teacher told me about the zeal my son demonstrated for writing computer programs. At first I was glad to see him zealously working at his computer. Unfortunately, he soon became so obsessed with the computer that he changed from a zealous student into a computer zealot who talked, thought, and dreamed nothing but computers. Political extremists who hi-jack airplanes are zealots who threaten passengers' lives.

*Synonyms:* enthusiastic, passionate, intense, earnest, ardent (AR dunt)

*Related words:* fervent, fervid, animated, indefatigable, assiduous, sedulous, diligent, impassioned, fanatic, fanatical, vehement, rabid

*Contrasted words:* apathetic, languorous, torpid, lethargic, phlegmatic, indolent, listless, dispassionate, indifferent, lackluster, lackadaisical, nonchalant, negligent

2. *candid* (KAN did) — honest, truthful, straightforward

The ancient Romans had two words for "white" — *albus* for ordinary white (from which comes our word "albumen," referring to the white of the egg) and *candidus* for shining white, as in the special gleaming white of new-fallen snow. *Candidus* was also associated with spotlessness and purity, as when referring to the honesty of one's character, the cleanness of one's writing style, or the beauty of one's features. Roman office seekers went among the public clad in white togas which symbolized their supposed honesty. They would even rub white chalk into their togas to further emphasize their pure, white, spotless integrity. From *candidatus* ("clothed in white") comes our word "candidate." We hope that our candidates are candid with us. However, a candidate who speaks with candor may not tell voters what they want to hear. Candid criticism may be helpful but not always pleasant, for "the truth hurts." *Candid Camera*, a T.V. show that made use of a hidden camera to catch the spontaneous, unposed, candid behavior of unsuspecting people, entertained viewers for many years.

*Synonyms:* sincere, direct, outspoken, frank, forthright, uninhibited (un in HIB ih tid)

*Related words*: blunt, forthright, unbiased, impartial, guileless, above-board

*Contrasted words:* evasive, biased, dissembling, deceitful, inhibited

3. *posthumous* (POS chuh mus) — occurring after death

"Posthumous" comes from Latin *postumus*, meaning "very last" (the superlative form of *post*, meaning "after"). Since an after-death occurrence is one which is the very last, *postumus* came to mean "after death." In Late Latin (approximately A.D. 200-600) *postumus* was written *posthumus*, since "after death" became associated with *post* ("after") and *humus* ("ground") — corpses being buried in the ground. Interestingly, the word "human" itself can be traced back to Indo-European (an ancient language from which Latin derived) *dhghem* ("earth"). In biblical Hebrew (which is not derived from Indo-European) the name *Adam* sounds like the Hebrew word for "earth"; thus the line from Genesis that reads "the Lord God formed man from the dust of the ground" (Gen. 2:7) reads in Hebrew something like this English equivalent: "God formed an earthling from the earth." The point is that both Hebrew and Indo-European languages associate the origin of man with the dust of the earth. Our life cycle as suggested by the etymologies of "human" and "posthumous" can be summarized in the familiar phrase "ashes to ashes and dust to dust." Today, "posthumous" refers to one born after a father's death, a work published after the author's death, and something surviving, continuing, or occurring after one's death. Ben Jonson, a contemporary of Shakespeare and author of the plays *Volpone* and *The Alchemist*, was a posthumous child, born one month after his father's death. Although Herman Melville, author of *Moby Dick*, died in 1891, his short novel *Billy Budd* was published posthumously in 1924. Not very well known at the time of his death, Melville has achieved great posthumous fame.

*Synonyms:* after-death, post-mortem (post MOR tum)

*Contrasted word:* prenatal

4. *enthrall* (en THRAWL) — charm, fascinate, please greatly

Orginally, "thrall" meant "slave" in English ("thralldom" still means "slavery"). To "enthrall" a person was to make that person a slave. Our modern dictionaries still list "enslave" as a meaning of "enthrall," though this meaning is used only rarely. Today when we are enthralled, we are metaphorically in bondage to that which greatly pleases or fascinates. Cleopatra enthralled Mark Antony. Sights such as India's beautiful Taj Mahal, Japan's sacred Mount Fuji, and Egypt's awesome pyramids enthrall tourists. Richard Wright's *Native Son*, Zora Neale Hurston's *Their Eyes Were Watching God*, Margaret Walker's *Jubilee*, and Alice Walker's *The Third Life of Grange Copeland* are powerful, enthralling novels about the Black American experience.

*Synonyms:* spellbind, thrill, enchant, captivate (KAP tuh vate)

*Related words:* allure, enrapture, bewitch, mesmerize, engross

5. *parasite* (PAR uh site) — plant or animal that lives on or in another and feeds off this other's body; a person receiving support without giving anything useful or meaningful in return

"Parasite" derives from Greek *para* ("beside") + *sitos* ("food," "grain"). Thus, the Greek *parasitos* was one who ate at the table of another, one who was literally beside the food. Originally, *parasitos* had a favorable meaning, for the term applied to priests, government officials, and heroes honored with a feast at the public expense. However, the custom was abused and *parasitos* became associated with guests who would flatter their hosts in order to be invited back for a free meal. From its original meaning of "table companion," *parasitos* came to mean an "insincere, flattering freeloader." Interestingly, the word "companion," from Latin *com* ("with") + *panis* ("bread"), has an etymology similar to "parasite" (*para* — "beside," *sitos* — "food," "grain"). Both words originally described people who ate with others. But whereas "companion" has retained a favorable meaning, "parasite" has degenerated to a term of contempt. Biologically, "parasite" refers to an organism that lives off of another, such as the fleas and worms that are parasites of dogs. Human parasites live at another's expense.

No one likes Uncle George, a parasite who only visits when he wants a free meal and a loan that he will never pay back. Mary should divorce her husband, a parasitic loafer who never works and spends almost all of her hard-earned money.

*Synonyms:* freeloader, deadbeat, sponger, sycophant (SIK uh funt)

*Related words:* leech, fawner, mendicant

6. *chagrin* (shuh GRIN) — humiliation, disappointment, irritation

We know that "chagrin" entered the English language from the French *chagrin* ("distressed"), but there is disagreement and uncertainty among etymologists about the earlier history of this word. There is a Turkish word *shagri*, meaning the "rump or hind part of a horse." From *shagri* comes a French word *chagrin*, meaning "rough leather or sharkskin." This rough material was used as an abrasive, as in rubbing the dirt off pots and pans. However, French *chagrin* also means "distressed." Chagrin ("distressed") does not derive from Turkish. Nevertheless, through association, the sense of the rough, irritating, abrasive nature of the Turkish-derived *chagrin* was probably transferred to the other chagrin ("distressed," "irritated"). Pardon the pun, but there may have been a rub-off effect of meaning. In any case, when we are "chagrined," we are irritated or rubbed the wrong way about something so that we feel saddened or disappointed. Much to my chagrin, I saw all my proposals rejected by other members of the committee. To his great chagrin, Napolean discovered that he could not conquer Russia.

*Synonyms:* shame, distress, embarrassment, mortification (mor tuh fuh KAY shun)

*Related words:* vexation, exasperation

*Contrasted words:* elation, exultation, jubilation, exhilaration, ecstasy

7. *cant* (KANT) — insincere talk; special language of a social class, trade, or profession

Cant derives from Latin *cantus* ("song"). Why would a word sprung from a song have a negative connotation? Evidently, people believed that some of the medieval clergymen who chanted their prayers were dully repetitious and insincere. Also, the beggars singing at church funeral services were viewed as insincere. These factors account for the negative meaning acquired by "cant" in English by the seventeenth century. Andrew Cant (1590-1663), a Scottish preacher notorious for viciously persecuting religious opponents while simultaneously praying for their souls, strengthened the negative overtone of "cant" by the word's association with his name. Dishonest, hypocritical, or flowery but empty speech — especially about ideals and religion — is cant. Be wary of the cant of politicians and preachers who are more concerned with fleecing than feeding their flock. "Cant" also refers to the special language of a group or profession. Economists and sociologists sometimes employ so much technical language or cant in T.V. interviews that the average person can't understand them.

*Synonyms:* insincerity, phoniness, empty talk, slang, technical language, jargon (JAR gun)

*Related words:* hypocrisy, sanctimoniousness, sanctimony, pretentious ness, sham, bombast, platitude, terminology, lingo, argot, parlance, patois, vernacular

8. *ephemeral* (ih FEM uh rul) — short-lived, fleeting, lasting a very short time

Ephemeral derives from Greek *epi* ("upon") and *hemera* ("day"). Hence, "ephemeral" refers to something that lasts only one day or passes quickly. The fame of best-sellers is ephemeral; most of us forget the names of best-sellers of only a few years ago. The Asian spiritual teacher Buddha emphasized the ever-changing, impermanent, ephemeral nature of existence. He saw that youth, health, and life itself rapidly vanish. The Englishman Robert Herrick (1591-1674) advised delighting in ephemeral pleasures:

> Gather ye rosebuds while ye may,
>     Old time is still a-flying;
> And this same flower that smiles today
>     Tomorrow will be dying.

*Synonyms:* momentary, brief, temporary, fading, transitory (TRAN suh tor ee)

*Related words:* evanescent, transient, unenduring, impermanent

*Contrasted words:* perpetual, abiding, enduring, interminable

9. *dexterous* (DEK stuh rus, DEK strus) — skillful, clever

10. *sinister* (SIN uh stur) — threatening, wicked, evil

Left-handers complain that this is a right-hander's world. Language supports the left-hander's complaint. We praise a good worker by calling him our "right-hand man"; no one likes receiving a "left-hand compliment." No wonder left-handers feel "left out." "Dexterous" comes from Latin *dexter* ("right," "right-hand") and "sinister" from Latin *sinister* ("left," "on the left-hand side"). Surgeons and pianists have manual dexterity. Clumsy dancers who are not dexterous are criticized as having two left feet. The threat of evil is associated with the left, for we refer to bloodcurdling howls accompanied by a sudden chill in the atmosphere as sinister events. Lord Acton noted the sinister nature of power, "Power tends to corrupt and absolute power corrupts absolutely." Edgar Allen Poe and Stephen King dexterously create sinister environments in their stories.

*Synonyms* for "dexterous": skilled, nimble, efficient, able, adroit (uh DROIT)

*Related words* for "dexterous": agile, deft, adept, facile, ingenious, proficient, resourceful

*Contrasted words* for "dexterous": inept, maladroit, gauche, ungainly

*Synonyms* for "sinister": menacing, frightening, unfavorable, villainous, treacherous, malevolent (muh LEV uh lunt)

*Related words* for "sinister": foreboding, ill-boding, ominous, inauspicious, unpropitious, portentious, vile, baleful, nefarious, iniquitous, malignant, perfidious, maleficent, heinous, depraved, malign, perverse, pernicious, deleterious

*Contrasted words* for "sinister": auspicious, innocuous, opportune, propitious, beneficent, benevolent, benign, felicitous

# Working With Words

*I. Fill in each blank with the appropriate word from the following list:*

parasites        zealously

dexterous      chagrin

posthumous    candid

enthralling     ephemeral

cant             sinister

*Each word must be used only once.*

The French writer Voltaire (1694-1778) (1)_____
attacked the stupidities and injustices of his time. Like his Anglo-Irish
contemporary Jonathan Swift (author of *Gulliver's Travels*), Voltaire
brilliantly employed satire — a literary form that ridicules society to
expose and, hopefully, to correct its faults — in his witty, delightful,
(2)_____ tale *Candide*. As his name suggests, Can-
dide — the hero of the novel — is indeed (3)_____
and honest. His truthfulness, innocence, and inexperience make him an
easy target for the scoundrels of the world. Forced to leave his
sweetheart and flee from Europe to the Americas, Candide soon ac-
quires an immense fortune. However, (4)_____
cluster around him wherever he goes so that his fortune quickly
dwindles. When he finally meets his long-lost love, Candide discovers,
much to his (5)_____, that his once enthralling
beloved has become an ugly, nagging wretch. Though beauty may be
(6)_____ and soon fade away, Candide steadfastly
holds to his sense of honor and marries her anyway. Through his skillful
and (7)_____ handling of the amusingly absurd inci-
dents in *Candide*, Voltaire entertains the reader while exposing
religious and political hypocrisy and (8)_____. In particular, Voltaire keenly satirizes the (9)_____, cruel,
and fanatically intolerant Inquisition that tortured its victims in the
name of God. Although Voltaire was immensely famous for a multitude
of works while he was alive, his (10)_____ fame rests
mainly on Candide.

## II. Match the word on the left with its synonyms.

___1. posthumous      a. jargon, empty talk

___2. parasite      b. captivate, enchant

___3. cant      c. transitory, momentary

___4. zealous      d. sycophant, freeloader

___5. dexterous      e. mortification, distress

___6. ephemeral      f. malevolent, menacing

___7. chagrin      g. adroit, skilled

___8. candid      h. post-mortem, after-death

___9. enthrall      i. ardent, enthusiastic

___10. sinister      j. uninhibited, sincere

## III. Word Part: BI — *two, twice (bicycle)*

*bilingual* (by LING gwul) — able to use two languages equally, or nearly equally, well; pertaining to, speaking, or written in two languages

*bigamy* (BIG uh mee) — marriage to two people at the same time

*biped* (BY ped) — two-footed animal

*bilateral* (by LAT uh rul) — having or concerning two sides, parties, countries, etc.

*bifocals* (by FOH kulz) — eyeglasses with lenses that have two sections for correcting both close and distant vision

*Using each of the five BI words only once, complete the following sentences.*

1. For the ten years that the traveling salesman had one wife in California and another wife in New York, neither his wives nor closest friends knew he was practicing _____ .

2. The U.S.A. and China reached a _____ trade agreement.

3. Thanks to Benjamin Franklin, the inventor of _____ ,
I need only one pair of glasses to correct my vision for both reading and distance.

4. The _____ guide spoke English and Spanish equally well.

5. The ostrich is a swift _____ , attaining speeds of forty miles per hour.

# Chapter 9

1. ignominy       6. indolent

2. aboveboard       7. meander

3. anecdote       8. precocious

4. bedlam       9. scapegoat

5. martinet       10. shibboleth

1. *ignominy* (IG nuh min ee) — disgrace, humiliation, shame

Oscar Wilde (1854-1900) wrote in his novel *The Picture of Dorian Gray*, "There is only one thing in the world worse than being talked about, and that is not being talked about." If we were without a name, it would be difficult for others to talk about us and for us to maintain our sense of identity. Losing our reputation or "good name," we lose an essential part of our being and identity. When ancient Romans suffered *ig-nominia* ("disgrace" or "dishonor"), they were "without" (*ig*) "name" (*nomen*), a condition that often drove them to suicide. Family names were restricted to the British upper classes until about the sixteenth century, so that to be without a family name was a sign of low status in the British social order. Today, "ignominy" refers to the dishonor and shame that often accompany loss of reputation or "good name." Judas bears the ignominy of betraying Christ. In some Muslim countries, criminals ignominiously suffer public punishment, such as the amputa-

tion of an arm for stealing. Shakespeare's Iago describes the ig-
nominious loss of one's good name in *Othello*:

> Good name in man and woman, dear my lord,
> Is the immediate jewel of their souls.
> Who steals my purse steals trash; tis something, noth
> ing;
> 'Twas mine, 'tis his, and has been slave to thousands;
> But he that filches from me my good name
> Robs me of that which not enriches him
> But makes me poor indeed.

*Synonyms:* dishonor, contempt, infamy (IN fuh mee)

*Related words:* obloquy, odium, opprobrium

*Contrasted words:* acclaim, commendation, esteem, veneration, adula
tion

2. *aboveboard* (uh BUV bord) — without dishonesty or trickery

Originally "aboveboard" was a gambler's term, referring to shuffling and
holding cards above the table or board (an early meaning for "board"
being "table," as can still be seen in the expressions "room and board"
and "chairman of the board"). Cheating was less likely when everyone's
cards and hands were in common view. Hence, today "aboveboard"
means "out in the open," "honest," "straightforward." "Aboveboard"
functions as both adjective and adverb. In our democratic society, we
want public officials to be sincere and aboveboard. If we discover that
officials have not been acting aboveboard with us, we may seek to
remove them from office. "Honesty is the best policy" counsels
aboveboard behavior.

*Synonyms:* forthright(ly), straightforward(ly), overt(ly) (oh VURT, OH
vurt)

*Related words:* frank(ly), candid(ly), veracious(ly), guileless(ly)

*Contrasted words:* covert(ly), clandestine(ly), furtive(ly), surreptitious(ly), devious(ly), mendacious(ly), guileful(ly), dissembling(ly)

3. *anecdote* (AN ik dote) — brief story of an interesting or amusing incident

During the sixth century A.D., the historian Procopius recorded life at the court of his master Justinian, emperor of the Byzantine Empire. Procopius included many sensational and indecent incidents, probably intending that his stories not be revealed to the public, for he titled them *Anecdota*, from Greek *an* ("not") + *ek* ("out") + *dotos* ("given"). However, these stories were too interesting to remain "not given out" and were eventually published after Procopius' death. Today, "anecdote" refers to any brief, often humorous tale. Walter Johnson, who pitched for the Washington Senators from 1907-1927, once had two strikes on a batter. The batter started walking away when the umpire called him back. "What's the use," responded the batter, "you can't hit what you can't see." This anecdote emphasizes the speed of Johnson's fastball.

*Synonyms:* sketch, fable, tale, narrative (NAR uh tiv)

*Related words:* yarn, reminiscence

4. *bedlam* (BED lum) — noisy confusion

In 1247 a building known as St. Mary of Bethlehem was erected in London to house members of a religious order. As part of the Protestant Reformation, King Henry VIII in 1536 closed most of the monasteries in England. St. Mary of Bethlehem was then converted into an insane asylum. In those days, visitors would tease and torment the inmates as if the inmates were wild, caged animals. The asylum became famous for its uproar and confusion. The word "Bethlehem" became contracted to "Bethlem" and eventually became pronounced and spelled "Bedlam." Because of its association with a noisy madhouse, "bedlam" has come into our language meaning "noisy disorder." The bedlam caused by their children's music and wild antics makes some parents wonder if their children are crazy or if their children will drive them crazy.

*Synonyms:* uproar, chaos, pandemonium (pan de MOH nee um)

*Related words:* tumult, turmoil, clamor

*Contrasted words:* serenity, repose, tranquility, placidness

5. *martinet* (mar tuh NET) — strict disciplinarian

During the reign of King Louis XIV of France, Colonel Martinet trained France's army. A fierce disciplinarian, he developed precise drills and permitted not the least deviance. Disliked by his men for his inflexible authority, Martinet nonetheless contributed to France's developing the best army in Europe. Martinet was "accidentally" killed by one of his own soldiers' bullets during a battle in 1672. His name lives on to describe unbending, almost fanatical authority.

　　Tough army sergeants and rigorous football coaches are martinets. Whereas some parents pamper and give in to their children, other parents are martinets who will not permit the slightest deviation from household rules.

*Synonyms:* taskmaster, slavedriver, authoritarian (uh thor uh TER ee un)

*Related words:* autocrat, tyrant, despot

*Contrasted words:* egalitarian, liberal, lenient person

6. *indolent* (IN duh lunt) — lazy

*Indolentia* was a Latin word meaning "freedom from pain," formed from *in* ("not") + *dolens* ("feeling pain"). *Indolentia* described the state of harmony or equilibrium attained when one is indifferent to the pleasures and pains of the world. When "indolence" entered English, it kept this spiritual or philosophical sense, meaning "a being insensible of pain or grief." "Indolent" also had the meaning of "painless" in this eighteenth-century citation from the *O.E.D.*: "An Indolent Tumor in her Breast!" Today, "indolent" has lost its sense of "indifferent to pain" (except in medical terminology where "indolent" still means "painless," as in "an indolent ulcer") and now means "indifferent to work or exertion." Indolent people would rather remain idle than be employed. Sunbathers indolently spend the day on the beach sipping cold drinks. Tennyson's poem "The Lotus-Eaters" describes the music that lulled Odysseus' men into indolence:

> Music that gentlier on the spirit lies,
> Than tired eyelids upon tired eyes;
> Music that brings sweet sleep down from the blissful
> skies.

*Synonyms:* idle, inactive, slothful (SLAWTH ful, SLOHTH ful)

*Related words:* inert, lethargic, listless, languid, lackadaisical, torpid

*Contrasted words:* diligent, assiduous, sedulous

7. **meander** (mee AN dur) — follow a winding course; wander idly or aimlessly

The ancient Greeks founded a city in Asia Minor called Miletus. Miletus was famous for its artists, writers, and thinkers. Thales of Miletus was a philospher, who, upon asked what was extremely difficult, answered, "To know thyself." In response to a question about what was very easy to do, he answered, "To give advice." Miletus was situated at the mouth of the river Meander. This river, now part of Turkey, was noted for its twisting, turning, winding course. According to the Latin poet Ovid, the Meander "flows backwards and forwards in its varying course and, meeting itself, beholds its waters that are to follow, until it fatigues its wandering current, now pointing to its source, and now to the open sea." Today, we meander when following curving, crooked, twisting paths — be they literal or figurative.

We lazily meandered in the woods, wandering without any set purpose other than to enjoy the sights of nature. While some people channel their energies and dedicate their lives to a definite goal, others meander their way through life, drifting in this direction, then that, appearing never to pursue anything in particular.

*Synonyms:* roam, rove, ramble, digress (dye GRES)

*Related words:* amble, zigzag, undulate

8. *precocious* (prih KOH shus) — advanced beyond one's age (especially in mental aptitude)

"Precocious" derives from Latin *prae* ("before") and *coquere* ("cook"). Latin *praecoquere* meant "cook beforehand" or "ripen beforehand." "Precocious" entered the English language to refer to flowers and fruits that ripened early. Now we apply "precocious" to children and youth whose mental or artistic qualities are far more developed than in others of their age. We sometimes hear of precocious mathematical wizards who enter college while other children of their age are still in elementary school. The precocious Mozart composed music at the age of five. English philosopher and economist John Stuart Mill (1806-1873) precociously learned Greek, Latin, algebra, and geometry by the age of eight. Of course, some precocious children may be heavily spoiled, making them atrocious.

*Synonyms:* smart, brilliant, gifted, characterizing a child prodigy (PROD uh jee)

9. *scapegoat* (SKAPE goat) — someone blamed for the faults of others

The high priest Aaron, brother of Moses, prepared one goat as a sacrifice for the Lord and symbolically put the sins of the Hebrews on a second goat, which he released into the wilderness. This second goat that escaped is called a "scapegoat" in the King James Version of the Bible (Leviticus XVI), "scape" being a shortened form of "escape." We are often tempted to simplify the cause of our problems and look for someone else to blame, making that person or group our scapegoat.

Adults who see all of their problems as stemming from their upbringing by their parents have made their parents into scapegoats.

Government officials become scapegoats when they unfairly receive the blame and punishment due their superiors.

*Synonyms:* victim, whipping boy

*Related words:* martyr, dupe

*Contrasted word:* malefactor

10. *shibboleth* (SHIB uh luth) — password, slogan, or custom characteristic of a certain group and used to distinguish that group; empty, outworn expression or doctrine

The Bible (Judges XII) recounts the war between Gilead and Ephraim. The warriors of Gilead captured the passages of the Jordan River. To prevent the soldiers of Ephraim from crossing the river, the guards of Gilead would ask anyone approaching them to say *shibboleth* (the Hebrew word for "stream" or "ear of corn"). The Ephraimites could not pronounce the "sh" sound and would say *sibboleth* instead of *shibboleth*. This mispronunciation revealed the true identity of the Ephraimites. In World War II, such words as "unintelligible" and "lollipop" were used by U.S. soldiers as shibboleths to reveal Japanese who were posing as friendly Chinese (the Japanese have great difficulty pronouncing "l," whereas the Chinese can pronounce "l" but have great difficulty pronouncing "r"). In addition to meaning "password," "shibboleth" also refers to stale expressions and ideas empty of true meaning. We tire of listening to the shibboleths of political parties, slogans that are no longer true and have lost their meaning. We must not be influenced by the shibboleths of racism and sexism if we are to judge people on their own merits.

*Synonyms:* peculiarity, catchword, watchword, platitude (PLAT uh tood)

*Related words:* banality, cliché, motto

# Working With Words

*I. Fill in each blank with the appropriate word from the following list:*

| | |
|---|---|
| indolent | precocious |
| aboveboard | anecdote |
| meander | ignominy |
| martinet | shibboleth |
| scapegoat | bedlam |

*Each word must be used only once.*

Whenever I recall my childhood visits during summer vacation to Uncle Ned — my father's youngest brother — I envision less a home than a military barracks. Uncle Ned was a fierce disciplinarian — a true (1)_____. We had no need for an alarm clock; Uncle Ned would bark orders for his children and me to get up at precisely 5:00 a.m. every morning. A rigidly structured day of assigned tasks would follow, interspersed with short, precisely timed periods of organized play. My easygoing father always looked upon his brother Ned with amused tolerance during these visits. Years later, after Uncle Ned had a fatal heart attack, my father told me this (2)_____ to explain my uncle's behavior. Ned had been a (3)_____ youth, reading novels by the time he was six and learning algebra at the age of eight. Being the youngest child and demonstrating the most academic potential, Ned was pampered and allowed to do much as he pleased. Not challenged at school, Ned grew bored, undisciplined, and lazy. He became so (4)_____ that in high school he would not bother to do routine homework assignments. Even though Ned did extremely well on the national standarized achievement tests — and received a scholarship from the college of his choice — he did not graduate from high school on schedule because he failed two required courses. When my grandparents learned of Ned's failure to graduate and subsequent loss of the scholarship, (5)_____ erupted in our household. Ned, formerly the pampered favorite, became the (6)_____ for any mishap in the house. If anything was wrong or not in its proper place — soiled laundry not in the hamper, dirty dishes left in the sink, even books not symmetrically shelved — my grandparents blamed Ned for shirking his chores and lectured him on the evils of indolence. They severely curtailed his free activities and no longer permitted him to either physically or intellectually (7)_____. Ned's parents dismissed the familar saying about all work and no play as an old (8)_____ irrelevant to his case. He was hounded to exactingly accomplish a barrage of household tasks — the Labors of Hercules were dwarfed by the labors of Ned. His parents monitored daily his academic progress as he repeated the two required high school courses. Of course, Uncle Ned eventually went on to college and became highly successful. The (9)_____ of his high school disaster, however, always remained with him. Therefore, although we knew him to be honest and (10)_____ with us — a man on whose word we could utterly count — we could also count on his fanatic devotion to discipline and order.

___1. meander

a. authoritarian, slavedriver

___2. aboveboard

b. whipping boy, victim

___3. scapegoat

c. characterizing a child prodigy, brilliant

___4. ignominy

d. slothful, idle

___5. shibboleth

e. infamy, dishonor

___6. bedlam

f. digress, roam

___7. precocious

g. narrative, tale

___8. martinet

h. platitude, watchword

___9. anecdote

i. pandemonium, chaos

___10. indolent

j. overt, straightforward

### III. Word Part: DUC — lead (introduce, reduce, educate)

*induce* (in DOOS) — persuade, bring about, cause

*seduce* (sih DOOS) — lead astray; persuade one to do wrong; persuade one to have sexual intercourse

*abduct* (ab DUKT) — carry off by force; kidnap

*traduce* (truh DOOS) — slander

*conducive* (kun DOO siv) — leading, contributing, promoting, helpful

**Using each of the five DUC words only once, complete the following sentences.**

1. The millionaire hired bodyguards because he feared kidnappers might _____ his children.

2. No tempting bribe could _____ the honest judge.

3. Fresh air, proper diet, moderate exercise, and relaxation are all _____ to good health.

4. Once she makes up her mind, nothing anyone says can _____ her to change it.

5. If you run for political office, you must expect that some of your opponents will try to _____ your character.

# Chapter 10

| | |
|---|---|
| 1. agnostic | 6. procrustean |
| 2. nepotism | 7. denigrate |
| 3. enigmatic | 8. prosaic |
| 4. blatant | 9. docile |
| 5. nebulous | 10. boycott |

1. *agnostic* (ag NOS tik) — one who believes it impossible to know whether or not God exists

The great British biologist Thomas Huxley defended Charles Darwin's theory of evolution so well that he was nicknamed "Darwin's bulldog." Tired of being called an "atheist" — "one who believes there is no God," from Greek *a* ("not") and *theos* ("god") — Huxley coined the word "agnostic" in 1869 to describe his position. Formed from Greek *a* ("not") and *gnosis* ("knowledge"), "agnostic" means a person who believes that we do not have the knowledge to know if there is or is not a God. The atheist denies the existence of God; the agnostic can neither affirm nor deny God's existence. A true agnostic response to the question "Does God exist?" would be "I don't know." Thomas Huxley, by the way, was the grandfather of the biologist Sir Julian Huxley and writer Aldous Huxley, author of *Brave New World*.

*Synonyms:* unbeliever, doubter, questioner, skeptic (SKEP tik)

2. *nepotism* (NEP uh tiz um) — favoritism to relatives in giving jobs and offices

In the early days of Christianity, Catholic priests sometimes married. So that priests would not be tempted to provide property and wealth for their offspring but would instead devote themselves totally to the Church, Pope Gregory VII forbade priests to marry in 1073. During the Middle Ages and Renaissance, however, many high church officials bestowed favors and offices on their illegitimate children. Because they could not lawfully recognize these offspring as their sons, the priests called them "nephews." From the Latin word for "nephew" — *nepos* — comes our word "nepotism," referring to favoritism toward relatives, especially in business and politics.

The boss who makes his incompetent son-in-law a top executive practices nepotism. Citizens may angrily denounce a mayor for nepotism if they discover he has appointed several relatives to high-salaried positions.

*Synonyms:* favoritism, patronage (PAY truh nij, PA truh nij)

3. *enigmatic* (en ig MAT ik) — puzzling, mysterious, perplexing

From the Greek *ainigma* ("riddle") derives our word "enigma." One of the most famous Greek riddles is the riddle of the Sphinx. The Sphinx — a winged creature with a lion's body, woman's head, and serpent's tail — would perch herself on a high boulder and ask travelers what walks on four legs in the morning, two legs in the afternoon, and three legs in the evening. If the travelers didn't know the answer, the Sphinx would eat them. No one made it past her until Oedipus arrived. He answered "man," since a baby crawls on fours, an adult walks on two legs, and an old person needs a cane. Stunned by this correct answer, the Sphinx suicidally hurled herself from the boulder. After solving the Sphinx's enigmatic question, Oedipus became King of Thebes and in the process of unraveling the enigma of his own birth discovered that he had killed his father and married his mother. Sophocles' play *Oedipus Rex* powerfully portrays this tragic story.

Sherlock Holmes could solve the most enigmatic crime. Winston Churchill said of Russia, "It is a riddle wrapped in a mystery inside an enigma."

*Synonyms:* mystifying, baffling, bewildering, obscure, cryptic (KRIP tik)

*Related words:* inexplicable, inscrutable, unintelligible, indecipherable, abstruse, equivocal

*Contrasted words:* candid, frank, intelligible, lucid

4. *blatant* (BLAYT unt) — completely obvious, often offensively so; shameless

In his poem *Faerie Queene*, Shakespeare's contemporary Edmund Spenser created the "Blatant Beast," who has a hundred tongues and a tail with a poisonous sting. The Blatant Beast symbolizes vicious, poisonous slander. Spenser probably coined "blatant" based on Latin *blaterare* ("babble"). Today, "blatant" has lost its monstrous association, but the word still often carries negative overtones. A blatant error is outstanding and obvious.

I found it blatantly apparent from the chocolate smudges on my children's faces that they had discovered the ice cream I brought home last night. Do you know anyone who can tell a bold-faced, brazen, blatant lie without blinking an eye?

*Synonyms:* clear, outstanding, prominent, conspicuous (kon SPIK yoo us)

*Related words:* overt, unsubtle, obtrusive, brazen, flagrant, egregious

*Contrasted words:* inconspicuous, subtle, unobtrusive

5. *nebulous* (NEB yuh lus) — unclear, hazy, indistinct

We certainly see clearer on a sunny day than a cloudy one. Since "nebulous" derives from Latin *nebula* ("cloud"), anything nebulous cannot be seen, understood, or penetrated clearly, as if it were wrapped in a cloudy mist. "Maybe" is a nebulous answer.

Doctors told the patient's family that the results of his medical tests were still too nebulous to determine treatment. Dark, cloudy skies made the prospect of a picnic nebulous. A nebula is a cloudlike patch of stars or gaseous matter.

*Synonyms:* fuzzy, murky, imprecise, confused, vague (VAYG)

*Related words:* indefinite, indeterminate, ambiguous, obscure, amorphous

*Contrasted words:* lucid, unambiguous

6. *procrustean* (pro KRUS tee un) — forcing rigid conformity

According to Greek mythology, Procrustes had a unique surprise for his victims. He would force them on an iron bed. If they were too long, he cut off part of their bodies; if they were too short, he stretched them to fit the bed. One size fatally fit all. Nowadays, "procrustean" applies to unyielding conformity. A wise instructor abhors forcing pupils on a Procrustean bed, realizing that some need to be gently led and coaxed while others need to be vigorously pushed and threatened. No procrustean authority would advocate "different strokes for different folks."

*Synonyms:* unyielding, inflexible, unbending, drastically rigid, ruthlessly rigid, stringent (STRIN junt)

*Related words:* obdurate, austere

*Contrasted words:* pliant, pliable, lax

7. *denigrate* (DEN uh grate) — defame, speak ill of, attack the reputation of

The negative connotation of "black" can be seen in such words as "blackball," "blacklist," and "blackmail." "Denigrate" derives from Latin *de* ("of") and *niger* ("black"). To denigrate someone's character is to blacken or attack it. During the Middle Ages and the Renaissance, the devil was commonly thought to be black. Shakespeare's villain Iago has this concept in mind when he asks "what delight shall she [Desdemona] have to look upon the devil," denigrating Desdemona's husband, the black general Othello, by equating him with the devil. Hopefully humans have progressed from linking skin with sin.

In a vicious political campaign, candidates often denigrate each other.

*Synonyms:* belittle, discredit, slander, disparage (dis PAR ij)

*Related words:* malign, vilify, sully, libel, calumniate, traduce

*Contrasted words:* extol, laud, exculpate, absolve, vindicate

8. *prosaic* (pro ZAY ik) — commonplace, dull, uninspired

"Prosaic" looks like "prose," and well it should, since "prosaic" derives from Latin *prosa* ("prose"). Common, normal, everyday activities are usually prosaic, as distinguished from colorful, exciting, poetic experiences. The seventeenth-century French comic genius Molière wrote the play *Le Bourgeois Gentilhomme* in which a character discovers that "for more than forty years I have been speaking prose without knowing it." Just as prose is our normal mode of expression, so our moment to moment daily existence is for the most part unspectacularly prosaic. In *Walden* Thoreau criticizes the prosaic, mechanical, uninspired routine of the majority, "The mass of men lead lives of quiet desperation." Of course, Thoreau led a simple, back to basics life at Walden Pond. However, his prose description of his life at Walden is not at all prosaic, rather an inspiring account of how nature can thrill the soul. Perhaps whether the world appears prosaic or poetic lies in the eyes of the beholder.

*Synonyms:* humdrum, uninteresting, ordinary, monotonous, mundane (mun DANE)

*Related words:* pedestrian, vapid, banal, trite, hackneyed

*Contrasted words:* lyrical, rapturous, fanciful

9. *docile* (DOS ul) — easily managed, controlled, or taught; gentle; submissive

Derived from Latin *docere* ("teach"), "doctor" originally referred to a teacher or any learned person. During the late Middle Ages, "doctor" began to designate more specifically someone practicing medicine. Etymologically akin to "doctor," "docile" means "easily taught or led."

Docile children easily submit to authority. The usually docile member surprised the committee by fiercely attacking the proposal. Although terrifying in appearance, the English bulldog makes a gentle, docile pet that will tolerate unlimited abuse from children. The bulldog is docile, not hostile.

*Synonyms:* obedient, manageable, amenable (uh MEE nuh bul, uh MEN uh bul)

*Related words:* tractable, compliant, pliant

*Contrasted words:* obdurate, truculent, refractory, fractious, contentious, belligerent, bellicose, pugnacious

10. *boycott* (BOY kot) — refuse to deal with as a means of protest and persuasion

In 1880 poor Irish tenants suffering from crop failure asked their local land agent, the retired English Army officer Captain Charles Cunningham Boycott, to lower their rents. Not only did Boycott deny their request, but he raised their rents. Angered, the tenants refused to pay him rent, stores would not sell to him, and roving bands prevented food supplies and mail from reaching him. Boycott fled for his life to England. Boycott's name quickly became synonymous for an act of protest in which the protestors refuse the goods and services of their opponent. "Boycott" can be either a noun or a verb. When a Black passenger named Rosa Parks was arrested in Montgomery, Alabama, in 1955 for breaking the city law requiring Blacks to sit or stand in the back of buses, Martin Luther King, Jr., organized a bus boycott. Blacks boycotted the buses until the U.S. Supreme Court ordered Montgomery to integrate its busing in 1956.

*Synonyms:* reject, ban, exclude, ostracize (OS truh size)

*Related words:* spurn, eschew, shun, abstain from, blacklist

*Contrasted word:* patronize

# Working With Words

*I. Fill in each blank with the appropriate word from the following list:*

enigma        docilely
boycott       blatantly
nebulous      agnostic
nepotism      procrustean
denigrating   prosaic

*Each word must be used only once.*

In the town of Unreel reigned mayor and corrupt political boss Louie Short. Because Short controlled the political structure of his town, he would (1)_____ disregard the normal legal procedures. He felt that such procedures were (2)_____ restrictions, conventional straitjackets that hindered his achieving his goals. Short's public displays of religious devotion helped maintain his popularity, although his private views about spiritual matters were unclear and (3)_____; in reality, he was an (4)_____ uncertain of God's existence. Short kept power by so savagely (5)_____ political opponents that his enemies usually (6)_____ submitted to his pressure rather than risk loss of their reputations. One man, however, refused to be intimidated. Quiet, conventional, (7)_____ in appearance, newspaper editor John Dull shocked everyone by attacking Mayor Short's nebulous handling of public funds, which was so vague and unclear as to make Short's handpicked government practically unaccountable for expenditures. The editor railed that financial administration should not be a puzzle, mystery, or (8)_____. Furthermore, Dull revealed the shocking extent of (9)_____, Short's blood relations or in-laws holding almost all government positions of any importance. Organizing a successful (10)_____ against businesses owned by Short and his relatives, John Dull accomplished what many thought impossible, not only removing Short from government but prompting the flight of the Shorts from the community.

## II. Match the word on the left with its synonyms.

___1. blatant      a. skeptic, unbeliever

___2. docile      b. cryptic, mystifying

___3. nepotism      c. conspicuous, prominent

___4. procrustean      d. vague, fuzzy

___5. denigrate      e. ostracize, reject

___6. agnostic      f. mundane, ordinary

___7. nebulous      g. patronage, favoritism

___8. boycott      h. amenable, obedient

___9. prosaic      i. stringent, inflexible

___10. enigmatic      j. disparage, slander

## III. Word Part: CARN — *flesh (carnation, carnival)*

*carnage* (KAR nij) — great slaughter, massacre

*carnal* (KAR nul) — pertaining to desires of the flesh; sensual, sexual, lustful, worldly

*carnivorous* (kar NIV ur us) — flesh-eating

*incarnate* (in KAR nit) — having bodily form, especially human form; personified

*reincarnation* (ree in kar NAY shun) — rebirth in another body

*Using each of the five CARN words only once, complete the following sentences.*

1. The kindly, unwordly, old philosopher felt few _____ desires.

2. Tigers, hawks, and sharks are _____.

3. In Shakespeare's *Othello*, the treacherously evil Iago appears to be the devil _____.

4. Do you believe that the remembering of past lives under hypnosis proves _____?

5. The great _____ at the Battle of Gettysburg moved Lincoln to deliver the Gettysburg Address.

# Master Exercises

*Select the definition closest in meaning in the following exercises.*

*I. This exercise reviews all words with a story.*

1. **aboveboard**
   (a) elevated
   (b) straightforward
   (c) rough
   (d) skillful

2. **aegis**
   (a) wisdom
   (b) hate
   (c) protection
   (d) passion

3. **agnostic**
   (a) doubter
   (b) actor
   (c) athlete
   (d) believer

4. **aloof**
   (a) lazy
   (b) soft
   (c) trustworthy
   (d) unconcerned

5. **amazon**
   (a) powerful woman
   (b) miracle
   (c) belief
   (d) troublesome child

6. **anecdote**
   (a) remedy
   (b) story
   (c) warrior
   (d) essence

7. **atone**
   (a) argue
   (b) speed up
   (c) slow down
   (d) make up for a wrong

8. **auspicious**
   (a) favorable
   (b) evil
   (c) protective
   (d) peculiar

9. **bedlam**
   (a) argument
   (b) revolution
   (c) contest
   (d) chaos

10. **blatant**
    (a) loud
    (b) confusing
    (c) obvious
    (d) quarrelsome

11. **bowdlerize**
    (a) delete
    (b) endanger
    (c) excite
    (d) hypnotize

12. **boycott**
(a) punish
(b) shorten
(c) endanger
(d) reject

13. **candid**
(a) tasty
(b) sweet
(c) clever
(d) honest

14. **cant**
(a) anger
(b) insincere talk
(c) journey
(d) danger

15. **capricious**
(a) jolly
(b) unpredictable
(c) honest
(d) loyal

16. **catholic**
(a) priestly
(b) universal
(c) sermonizing
(d) humble

17. **chagrin**
(a) joy
(b) disappointment
(c) excitement
(d) laziness

18. **cupidity**
(a) love
(b) greed
(c) intelligence
(d) archery

19. **curtail**
(a) lengthen
(b) shorten
(c) stretch
(d) tighten

20. **cynical**
(a) bold
(b) respectful
(c) distrustful
(d) cautious

21. **decimate**
(a) destroy
(b) dedicate
(c) calculate
(d) punish

22. **denigrate**
(a) praise
(b) correct
(c) explain
(d) slander

23. **dexterous**
(a) tricky
(b) skillful
(c) decisive
(d) undisciplined

24. **diffident**
(a) faithful
(b) confident
(c) timid
(d) daring

25. **docile**
(a) gentle
(b) fat
(c) strong
(d) stubborn

26. **egregious**
    (a) outrageous    (b) vague
    (c) soothing    (d) precise

27. **enigmatic**
    (a) puzzling    (b) energetic
    (c) lazy    (d) brave

28. **enthrall**
    (a) throw    (b) catch
    (c) fascinate    (d) weaken

29. **ephemeral**
    (a) transparent    (b) lifeless
    (c) momentary    (d) dull

30. **erotic**
    (a) nervous    (b) obscene
    (c) exciting    (d) sexual

31. **expedite**
    (a) prohibit    (b) allow
    (c) slow down    (d) speed up

32. **extrovert**
    (a) shy person    (b) outgoing person
    (c) wise person    (d) criminal

33. **fiasco**
    (a) party    (b) chaos
    (c) committee    (d) failure

34. **foible**
    (a) sharp point    (b) dull point
    (c) servant    (d) fault

35. **forte**
    (a) armor    (b) soldier
    (c) peculiarity    (d) strong point

36. **galvanize**
    (a) excite    (b) dull
    (c) wander    (d) defend

37. **gregarious**
    (a) dirty    (b) clever
    (c) calm    (d) sociable

38. **haggard**
    (a) ugly    (b) weary
    (c) playful    (d) serious

39. **havoc**
    (a) support    (b) anger
    (c) destruction    (d) irritation

40. **herculean**    (a) bloody    (b) confused
   (c) mighty    (d) fantasy

41. **hypocrisy**    (a) ruler    (b) industriousness
   (c) insincerity    (d) tyrant

42. **iconoclast**    (a) rebel    (b) oppressor
   (c) master    (d) leader

43. **idiosyncrasy**    (a) peculiarity    (b) handicap
   (c) deformity    (d) advantage

44. **ignominy**    (a) reward    (b) punishment
   (c) honor    (d) disgrace

45. **impede**    (a) delay    (b) torture
   (c) promote    (d) travel

46. **incumbent**    (a) deadly    (b) sleepily
   (c) hypnotic    (d) required

47. **indolent**    (a) energetic    (b) lazy
   (c) clever    (d) foolish

48. **introvert**    (a) shy person    (b) socializer
   (c) dictator    (d) slave

49. **jaded**    (a) tired out    (b) precious
   (c) expensive    (d) attractive

50. **jeopardize**    (a) strangle    (b) endanger
   (c) wound    (d) drown

51. **jovial**    (a) watery    (b) rough
   (c) divine    (d) jolly

52. **labyrinth**    (a) maze    (b) discipline
   (c) uproar    (d) scientific

53. **laconic**    (a) huge    (b) savage
   (c) brief    (d) playful

54. **lethargic**

(a) painful     (b) soothing
(c) lazy     (d) effective

55. **lewd**

(a) short     (b) uncertain
(c) indecent     (d) fierce

56. **Machiavellian**

(a) supportive     (b) quiet
(c) crafty     (d) slanderous

57. **martial**

(a) astronomical     (b) distant
(c) pleasant     (d) warlike

58. **martinet**

(a) manager     (b) athlete
(c) politician     (d) disciplinarian

59. **maudlin**

(a) sentimental     (b) religious
(c) proud     (d) fanatical

60. **meander**

(a) correct     (b) cheat
(c) wander     (d) infect

61. **mentor**

(a) guide     (b) enemy
(c) student     (d) lover

62. **mercurial**

(a) steady     (b) unstable
(c) positive     (d) warm

63. **mesmerize**

(a) soothe     (b) hypnotize
(c) rebel     (d) trick

64. **narcissism**

(a) wealth     (b) obscenity
(c) self-love     (d) generosity

65. **nebulous**

(a) concentrated     (b) weak
(c) warlike     (d) unclear

66. **nemesis**

(a) happiness     (b) entertainment
(c) idealism     (d) downfall

67. **nepotism**

(a) dictatorship     (b) favor to relatives
(c) charity     (d) scandal

68. **odyssey**        (a) battle          (b) journey
                       (c) contest         (d) suffering

69. **ostracize**      (a) win             (b) elect
                       (c) reject          (d) hypnotize

70. **panacea**        (a) poverty         (b) warning
                       (c) destruction     (d) remedy

71. **pandemonium**    (a) chaos           (b) conference
                       (c) zoo             (d) university

72. **pander**         (a) stir up hate    (b) play up to desires
                       (c) speak softly    (d) spread lies

73. **parasite**       (a) freeloader      (b) teacher
                       (c) aristocrat      (d) artist

74. **philistine**     (a) barbarian       (b) priest
                       (c) intellectual    (d) soldier

75. **posthumous**     (a) earthly         (b) heavenly
                       (c) after-death     (d) newborn

76. **precarious**     (a) religious       (b) sacred
                       (c) safe            (d) hazardous

77. **precocious**     (a) awkward         (b) advanced in development
                       (c) confident       (d) shameful

78. **prevaricate**    (a) delay           (b) harm
                       (c) mislead         (d) banish

79. **procrastinate**  (a) feast           (b) create
                       (c) argue           (d) delay

80. **procrustean**    (a) protective      (b) soft
                       (c) inflexible      (d) supportive

81. **prosaic**        (a) imaginative     (b) terrifying
                       (c) ordinary        (d) unhealthy

82. **protean**
    (a) nutritious  (b) false
    (c) happy  (d) changeable

83. **quintessence**
    (a) summary  (b) slander
    (c) essence  (d) praise

84. **quixotic**
    (a) idealistic  (b) faithful
    (c) argumentative  (d) deadly

85. **rankle**
    (a) irritate  (b) explain
    (c) praise  (d) sharpen

86. **sardonic**
    (a) comforting  (b) sad
    (c) unexpected  (d) mocking

87. **saturnine**
    (a) holy  (b) fashionable
    (c) gloomy  (d) dizzy

88. **scapegoat**
    (a) oppressor  (b) victim
    (c) conqueror  (d) servant

89. **scruple**
    (a) joke  (b) speech
    (c) prediction  (d) conscience

90. **shibboleth**
    (a) slogan  (b) sacrifice
    (c) tent  (d) feast

91. **sinister**
    (a) related  (b) wicked
    (c) magical  (d) ordinary

92. **stigma**
    (a) spear  (b) statement
    (c) stain  (d) song

93. **stoical**
    (a) uncertain  (b) bloody
    (c) sickly  (d) self-controlled

94. **succinct**
    (a) brief  (b) sweet
    (c) juicy  (d) bold

95. **succumb**
    (a) succeed  (b) remove
    (c) examine  (d) surrender

96. **supercilious**      (a) scornful        (b) silly
                          (c) powerful        (d) flattering

97. **tantalize**         (a) cheat           (b) tease
                          (c) explain         (d) criticize

98. **travesty**          (a) lecture         (b) joke
                          (c) work            (d) vacation

99. **utopian**           (a) united          (b) visionary
                          (c) clean           (d) complicated

100. **zealous**          (a) hopeful         (b) unfortunate
                          (c) unsure          (d) enthusiastic

*II. Review of all the synonyms that were reinforced by exercises in the individual chapters.*

1. **adroit**
   (a) dwarfish
   (b) gigantic
   (c) nonsensical
   (d) skillful

2. **amatory**
   (a) loving
   (b) hateful
   (c) pleasing
   (d) restless

3. **amenable**
   (a) obnoxious
   (b) agreeable
   (c) upset
   (d) thankful

4. **animate**
   (a) degrade
   (b) shout at
   (c) enliven
   (d) succeed

5. **ardent**
   (a) difficult
   (b) stiff
   (c) passionate
   (d) ignorant

6. **auspices**
   (a) promise
   (b) explanation
   (c) sponsorship
   (d) attack

7. **authoritarian**
   (a) singer
   (b) lawyer
   (c) messenger
   (d) disciplinarian

8. **avarice**
   (a) anger
   (b) irritableness
   (c) shyness
   (d) greed

9. **bellicose**
   (a) ringing
   (b) combative
   (c) spiritual
   (d) greedy

10. **boor**
    (a) pig
    (b) rude person
    (c) program
    (d) humble person

11. **capitulate**
    (a) support
    (b) surrender
    (c) overwhelm
    (d) study

12. **captivate**
    (a) fight
    (b) lose faith
    (c) make peace
    (d) enchant

13. **cater**
    (a) gratify
    (b) connect
    (c) demonstrate
    (d) punish

14. **chimerical**     (a) fanciful          (b) horrible
                       (c) musical           (d) numerous

15. **colossal**       (a) immense           (b) talented
                       (c) costly            (d) impractical

16. **conspicuous**    (a) obvious           (b) unknown
                       (c) hidden            (d) dependent

17. **conundrum**      (a) puzzle            (b) container
                       (c) dwelling          (d) weapon

18. **convivial**      (a) sociable          (b) sly
                       (c) disloyal          (d) powerful

19. **cryptic**        (a) sentimental       (b) sacred
                       (c) mysterious        (d) dirty

20. **debacle**        (a) failure           (b) success
                       (c) freedom           (d) slavery

21. **defer**          (a) postpone          (b) insure
                       (c) irritate          (d) cure

22. **derisive**       (a) pleasant          (b) untidy
                       (c) magnificent       (d) ridiculing

23. **devastation**    (a) entrance          (b) palace
                       (c) creation          (d) ruin

24. **digress**        (a) eject             (b) place
                       (c) wander            (d) attack

25. **diminish**       (a) express           (b) lift
                       (c) lessen            (d) reward

26. **disparage**      (a) delay             (b) belittle
                       (c) accumulate        (d) praise

27. **dissenter**      (a) messenger         (b) rebel
                       (c) laborer           (d) remedy

**28. duplicity**
(a) deception (b) truth
(c) nearness (d) skill

**29. eccentricity**
(a) peculiarity (b) safety
(c) generosity (d) wisdom

**30. egoism**
(a) health (b) wealth
(c) conceit (d) skill

**31. enthrall**
(a) scold (b) notice
(c) introduce (d) fascinate

**32. entice**
(a) enter (b) exit
(c) tempt (d) discourage

**33. equivocate**
(a) equalize (b) distribute
(c) return (d) be ambigious

**34. erratic**
(a) sensible (b) intuitive
(c) unpredictable (d) common

**35. exasperate**
(a) investigate (b) irritate
(c) promote (d) weaken

**36. expiate**
(a) lose (b) make amends for
(c) dismiss (d) nourish completely

**37. expurgate**
(a) explode (b) teach
(c) delete (d) copy

**38. facilitate**
(a) forbid (b) destroy
(c) demand (d) help accomplish

**39. flagrant**
(a) fearful (b) impossible
(c) outrageous (d) modest

**40. gaunt**
(a) happy (b) short and sweet
(c) fat and tall (d) grim and lean

**41. gregarious person**
(a) beggar (b) coward
(c) widow (d) socializer

42. **guileful**      (a) calm              (b) deceitful
                      (c) hasty             (d) unconscious

43. **haughty**       (a) protective        (b) proud
                      (c) peaceful          (d) fascinating

44. **imperil**       (a) endanger          (b) marry royalty
                      (c) exclude           (d) encourage

45. **imperturbable** (a) confused          (b) self-controlled
                      (c) joyous            (d) early

46. **indifferent**   (a) unconcerned       (b) untrue
                      (c) unusable          (d) unsure

47. **infamy**        (a) fortune           (b) conscience
                      (c) dishonor          (d) respect

48. **infirmity**     (a) weakness          (b) strength
                      (c) humor             (d) seriousness

49. **jargon**        (a) slang             (b) humor
                      (c) clown             (d) destruction

50. **jocular**       (a) hot               (b) jolly
                      (c) hot-tempered      (d) quiet

51. **lascivious**    (a) lustful           (b) graceful
                      (c) obedient          (d) popular

52. **malevolent**    (a) evil              (b) helpful
                      (c) trustworthy       (d) cowardly

53. **mawkish**       (a) brave             (b) sentimental
                      (c) cowardly          (d) decisive

54. **métier**        (a) conductor         (b) teacher
                      (c) enemy             (d) special skill

55. **morose**        (a) gloomy            (b) practical
                      (c) visionary         (d) precise

56. **mortification**

(a) incident     (b) distress

(c) understanding     (d) concentration

57. **mundane**

(a) soiled     (b) pure

(c) ordinary     (d) spectacular

58. **narrative**

(a) story     (b) pain

(c) ridicule     (d) opportunity

59. **nostrum**

(a) darkness     (b) alcoholic beverage

(c) jail     (d) remedy

60. **obligatory**

(a) clean     (b) required

(c) beautiful     (d) pleasing

61. **ostracize**

(a) run away     (b) show fear

(c) reject     (d) welcome

62. **overt**

(a) concealed     (b) clearly apparent

(c) sleepy     (d) fully automatic

63. **pandemonium**

(a) chaos     (b) passion

(c) lie     (d) athletic woman

64. **paragon**

(a) slave     (b) delicious fruit

(c) speech     (d) model

65. **parody**

(a) prose     (b) poetry

(c) mockery     (d) display

66. **patronage**

(a) success     (b) guest

(c) garbage     (d) support

67. **peregrination**

(a) communication     (b) flock of birds

(c) journey     (d) sickness

68. **perilous**

(a) unsafe     (b) sexy

(c) calm     (d) rapid

69. **platitude**

(a) refuge     (b) empty expression

(c) joke     (d) powerful ruler

70. **post-mortem**
(a) late
(b) responsible
(c) after-death
(d) youthful

71. **preceptor**
(a) example
(b) teacher
(c) feast
(d) garbage

72. **prodigy**
(a) gifted child
(b) moron
(c) wise man
(d) witch

73. **propitious**
(a) spoiled
(b) refreshing
(c) favorable
(d) unnatural

74. **qualm**
(a) uproar
(b) slaughter
(c) riddle
(d) misgiving

75. **ravage**
(a) flood
(b) quicken
(c) enforce
(d) destroy

76. **retribution**
(a) punishment
(b) promotion
(c) journey
(d) flatterer

77. **satiated**
(a) recognized
(b) punished
(c) successful
(d) overindulged

78. **self-scrutinizer**
(a) torturer
(b) self-examiner
(c) sick person
(d) selfish person

79. **shun**
(a) solve
(b) argue
(c) debate
(d) reject

80. **skeptic**
(a) liar
(b) doubter
(c) traitor
(d) supporter

81. **slothful**
(a) lazy
(b) energetic
(c) pure
(d) corrupted

82. **stringent**
(a) strict
(b) stable
(c) stubborn
(d) silent

83. **sycophant**
(a) flatterer
(b) teacher
(c) critic
(d) rebel

84. **taint**
    (a) stain
    (b) contradiction
    (c) criticism
    (d) punishment

85. **terse**
    (a) lengthy
    (b) silly
    (c) brief
    (d) overpowering

86. **thwart**
    (a) block
    (b) help
    (c) develop
    (d) imitate

87. **timorous**
    (a) brave
    (b) wealthy
    (c) timid
    (d) loud

88. **torpid**
    (a) sluggish
    (b) exciting
    (c) questioning
    (d) military

89. **transitory**
    (a) temporary
    (b) adventurous
    (c) unpractical
    (d) useful

90. **tumult**
    (a) mixture
    (b) noisy confusion
    (c) fashion
    (d) loud speech

91. **unbiased**
    (a) unprejudiced
    (b) unfair
    (c) disturbed
    (d) unknown

92. **unfeasible**
    (a) impractical
    (b) impulsive
    (c) lazy
    (d) inaccurate

93. **uninhibited**
    (a) protective
    (b) straightforward
    (c) silly
    (d) anxious

94. **vague**
    (a) unclear
    (b) important
    (c) heavenly
    (d) practical

95. **versatile**
    (a) variable
    (b) wonderful
    (c) unbelieveable
    (d) entertaining

96. **virago**
    (a) hurricane
    (b) rebellious youth
    (c) earthquake
    (d) ill-tempered woman

97. **whimsical**
    (a) impulsive
    (b) delirious
    (c) unusual
    (d) serious

98. **whipping boy**    (a) tyrant         (b) victim
                        (c) adolescent     (d) jockey

*III.* *This exercise reviews those words which were derived from the word parts at the end of the individual chapters.*

1. **abduct**
   (a) drop     (b) contact
   (c) reduce     (d) kidnap

2. **antipathy**
   (a) dislike     (b) cure
   (c) relation     (d) explanation

3. **apathetic**
   (a) beautiful     (b) unconcerned
   (c) sad     (d) happy

4. **avocation**
   (a) hobby     (b) pilot
   (c) calculation     (d) belief

5. **benediction**
   (a) blessing     (b) curse
   (c) misfortune     (d) kind ruler

6. **benefactor**
   (a) oppressor     (b) servant
   (c) helper     (d) guest

7. **beneficiary**
   (a) receiver     (b) donor
   (c) passenger     (d) citizen

8. **beneficence**
   (a) evil     (b) goodness
   (c) disease     (d) health

9. **benevolent**
   (a) fat     (b) thin
   (c) kind     (d) cruel

10. **bigamy**
    (a) growth     (b) nutrition
    (c) size     (d) having two mates

11. **bifocals**
    (a) windows     (b) type of eyeglasses
    (c) partnership     (d) monument

12. **bilateral**
    (a) promising     (b) having two wheels
    (c) pleasant     (d) two-sided

13. **bilingual**
    (a) balanced     (b) using two languages
    (c) unholy     (d) double-edged

14. **biped**
(a) human
(b) insect
(c) statue
(d) two-footed animal

15. **carnage**
(a) royalty
(b) flower
(c) massacre
(d) industry

16. **carnal**
(a) spiritual
(b) bloody
(c) pleasant
(d) sensual

17. **carnivorous**
(a) real
(b) false
(c) flesh-eating
(d) artistic

18. **circumspect**
(a) lonely
(b) careful
(c) unavoidable
(d) accidental

19. **conducive**
(a) contributing
(b) failing
(c) controlling
(d) wishing

20. **empathize**
(a) hate
(b) attack
(c) shut down
(d) identify with

21. **equivocate**
(a) travel
(b) shout
(c) hedge
(d) build

22. **eugenics**
(a) peace
(b) generosity
(c) crime
(d) selective breeding

23. **eulogy**
(a) misfortune
(b) slow growth
(c) praise
(d) rapid development

24. **euphemism**
(a) hobby
(b) mild expression
(c) instructor
(d) child genius

25. **euphoria**
(a) food
(b) great happiness
(c) vacation
(d) unexpected event

26. **euthanasia**
(a) mercy killing
(b) ideal government
(c) slaughter
(d) excitement

27. **evocative**
(a) suggestive
(b) necessary
(c) disrespectful
(d) unknown

28. **incarnate**
(a) lack of space
(b) having bodily form
(c) furious
(d) without permission

29. **induce**
(a) cause
(b) stop
(c) slow down
(d) kill

30. **introspective**
(a) fortunate
(b) seeking success
(c) comical
(d) looking inward

31. **irrevocable**
(a) successful
(b) strict
(c) unchangeable
(d) unfaithful

32. **malady**
(a) money
(b) harmony
(c) disorder
(d) high official

33. **malefactor**
(a) hero
(b) celebrity
(c) criminal
(d) instructor

34. **malice**
(a) amusement
(b) luxury
(c) ill will
(d) sexual assualt

35. **malinger**
(a) complain
(b) study
(c) shirk
(d) travel

36. **malpractice**
(a) education
(b) discipline
(c) truth
(d) misconduct

37. **monogamy**
(a) drowsiness
(b) marriage to one mate
(c) big business
(d) total control

38. **monologue**
(a) dream
(b) single parent
(c) invention
(d) speech

39. **monopoly**
(a) holiday
(b) sermon
(c) relationship
(d) total control

40. **monotheism**
(a) childhood
(b) worship of nature
(c) dictatorship
(d) belief in one god

41. **monotonous**
(a) dull
(b) colorful
(c) whispering
(d) informative

42. **pathos**    (a) sadness    (b) pathway
     (c) priest    (d) servant

43. **prospective**    (a) exact    (b) potential
     (c) magnificent    (d) plentiful

44. **psychopath**    (a) leader    (b) defense attorney
     (c) judge    (d) unstable person

45. **reincarnation**    (a) overproduction    (b) rebirth
     (c) foundation    (d) creativity

46. **retrospective**    (a) unhealthy    (b) looking backward
     (c) examining    (d) preventing

47. **seduce**    (a) promote    (b) show by example
     (c) be fashionable    (d) lead astray

48. **specious**    (a) satisfying    (b) misleading
     (c) terrifying    (d) protective

49. **traduce**    (a) support    (b) ignore
     (c) slander    (d) inflict punishment

50. **vociferous**    (a) quiet    (b) nonsensical
     (c) noisy    (d) elegant

# BIBLIOGRAPHY

Most collegiate and unabridged dictionaries provide etymologies for words. Enclosed in brackets, these etymologies either precede or follow the definition. I particularly like the etymologies in *Webster's New World Dictionary* and the first edition of *The American Heritage Dictionary*. Space limitations, however, necessitate that dictionary etymologies be extremely compressed. There are also three standard modern etymological dictionaries: *Klein's Comprehensive Etymological Dictionary of the English Language, Origins — A Short Etymological Dictionary of Modern English*, and *The Oxford Dictionary of English Etymology*. The etymologies in these dictionaries are also compressed rather than narrative. The *Oxford English Dictionary* stands in a class by itself. It is a monumental work that contains a wealth of contextual illustrations to trace the evolution of words. Anyone interested in words should become acquainted with this work. What follows is a partial list of popular books that leisurely and entertainingly present fascinating etymologies for the general reader.

The American Heritage Dictionary Editors. *Word Mysteries & Histories*. Boston: Houghton Mifflin Company, 1986.

Asimov, Issac. *Words from History*. Boston: Houghton Mifflin Company, 1968.

Ciardi, John. *A Browser's Dictionary*. New York: Harper and Row, 1980.

_____. *Good Words to You*. New York: Harper and Row, 1987.

_____. *A Second Browser's Dictionary*. New York: Harper and Row, 1983.

Evans, Ivor H., ed. *Brewer's Dictionary of Phrases & Fables*. New York: Harper and Row, 1981.

Freeman, Morton S. *The Story Behind the Word*. Philadelphia: ISI Press, 1985.

Funk, Charles Earle. *Thereby Hangs a Tale*. New York: Harper & Row, 1950.

Funk, Wilfred. *Word Origins and Their Romantic Stories*. New York: Bell Publishing Company, 1950.

Heller, Louis G., Alexander Humez, and Malcah Dror. *The Private Lives of English Words*. Detroit: Gale Research Company, 1984.

Hendrickson, Robert. *The Dictionary of Eponyms*. New York: Stein and Day, 1985.

Morris, William and Mary Morris. *Morris Dictionary of Word and Phrase Origins*. New York: Harper and Row, 1977.

Shipley, Joseph T. *Dictionary of Word Origins*. Totowa, NJ: Littlefield, Adams, and Company, 1967.

# Index

Words with exercises are in *italics*; the 100 core words are in **boldface**.